Rewriting NETWORK NEWS

WordWatching Tips from 345 TV and Radio Scripts

Mervin Block

Bonus Books, Inc., Chicago

94 93 92 91 90 5 4 3 2 1

International Standard Book Number: 0-929387-15-5
Library of Congress 90-80011

Bonus Books, Inc.
160 East Illinois Street
Chicago, Illinois 60611

Printed in the United States of America

My warmest thanks to Julia B. Hall, whose fine editing helped this book greatly.

The wise course is to profit from the mistakes of others.

Terence (Roman writer)

We often discover what *will* do by finding out what will not do.

Samuel Smiles

Intelligence is not to make no mistakes but quickly to see how to make them good.

Bertolt Brecht

There is nothing wrong with making mistakes. Just don't respond with encores.

Anon.

Anyone can make a mistake, and everyone does. But smart writers make the most of their mistakes—by learning all they can from them.

Newswriters are especially vulnerable. We often work amid frenzy: producers screaming, reporters scrambling, audio blaring. And through this bedlam, we must fight deadlines, balance the *diktats* of our bosses with the dictates of journalism—and write.

We do the best we can. But if we trip or flop, we try to do better next time. One way to improve is to find out where our scripts have gone wrong—and what to do about them. When we see what *not* to do, we move toward a grasp of what *to* do. So a study of mistakes can lead to better writing.

Though mistakes are often our best teachers, no one has awarded prizes for the most memorable mistakes of the year. The Museum of Broadcasting hasn't showcased mistakes. And no one has published a collection of faulty news scripts. Writers have had no opportunity to learn from a broad range of other newswriters' mistakes—until now. To help meet the need, this book provides examples from several hundred flawed scripts, plus corrections, comments and suggestions for improvement.

These examples feature problems in grammar, news judgment, broadcast style and storytelling. Almost all the scripts were broadcast by a network, but they could just as easily have popped up elsewhere. Anywhere. Wherever we turn.

I wince so often when I hear newscasts that my friends think I have a tic. Wince cometh my affliction? From the mistakes that shower down on us. A veritable rain of error.

How do so many mistakes get on the air? Easily; a writer's mistake slips past two or three staff members who process copy. And other newspeople who don't know any better accept what they hear on air as correct—and perpetuate those mistakes.

In an effort to cut down on mistakes and improve writing, CBS News hired me in 1977 to review all network scripts, radio and television. The news division issued a memo informing the staff that I was undertaking a one-month experiment to go over scripts that had been broadcast. "His effort," the memo said, ". . . will be to aid us all in raising the quality of our editorial product to an even higher level. . . ."[1]

Each day, I waded through as many scripts and transcripts as possible and photocopied about twenty pages that had mistakes or something especially good. Then I underlined or circled the pertinent word or passage and wrote a memo to the writer.

In addition, I wrote a weekly two-page newsletter with a roundup of hits and errors. The writers of praiseworthy scripts were identified. But writers of scripts requiring first aid, or surgery, were not identified. The newsletter was called *Second Look.*[2] In the first issue, I said I would work on the sidelines, away from deadlines and headlines, and would read scripts with the acuity of hindsight. The project's intention was to spotlight sins, not sinners.

My memos, reprinted in this book, pinpoint the same kinds of mistakes we hear today. Every day. Day after day. On radio and television. Local and network. Even on the best newscasts.

The frequency of these mistakes helps make the following pages—scripts, plus memos and new suggestions—evergreen. Incidentally, as anchors say when

1. CBS Memorandum, Jan. 7, 1977. The memo, addressed to all personnel in the news division, is reprinted in Appendix A.

2. The name was suggested by Norman Glubok, an associate producer on the "CBS Morning News." The final issue, dated Feb. 4, 1977, is shown in Appendix B.

introducing an item not at all incidental, three of the best books on writing are more than a half-century old. *The Elements of Style* was published in 1919. Forty years later, the book by William Strunk, Jr., was revised by E. B. White. Even now, Strunk and White's book is still printed, still widely read, still as good as the day it was born. Another classic, *The Golden Book on Writing* by David Lambuth, was published in 1923. It's reprinted, and shines with its original luster. And H. W. Fowler's *Modern English Usage* was published in 1926. Revised in 1965, it's still referred to and revered.

I'm not comparing this work to those masterworks, but I hope writers will find the following scripts and memos timely and helpful. The scripts or excerpts are printed in this typeface. The word or words to which my memo was directing the writer's attention are underlined. I also use this method in newswriting workshops at radio and television stations.

I don't identify writers who've erred or their stations, but I'm departing from that policy here because the *Second Look* project is public knowledge. It was first mentioned in a newspaper article[3], later in a book about television[4] and recently in a journalism textbook.[5] So in this book, I identify the source of scripts but not the writers.

In addition to those scripts, I'm reprinting some post-*Second Look* scripts, network and local, because their mistakes are instructive. You'll find these new scripts in this typeface.

My *Second Look* memos are reprinted word for word in this typeface.

---

3. Edwin Diamond, "Every Medium Needs Editors," *New York Times*, Aug. 26, 1979, D 29. The article is reprinted in Appendix C.

4. Edwin Diamond, *Sign Off: The Last Days of Television* (Cambridge: M.I.T. Press, 1982), 10.

5. Mitchell Stephens, *Broadcast News* (New York: Holt, Rinehart and Winston), 18, 36, 44, 60, 62, 103.

In many cases, I've added to what I wrote back then; these new comments are printed in this typeface. In a few cases, I've reworded what I wrote then (and identified the revision). After all, I try to learn from my mistakes.

Absolutes

"The schools are expected to remain closed at least through tomorrow, but the critical shortage of natural gas here is a problem that won't go away until the unprecedented cold spell ends."

"Unprecedented" and other absolutes, such as "first," "biggest," "unique," etc., are dangerous to use. Although yesterday's low in Kansas City was -7, the temperature hit -11 on Dec. 31, and even that was not unprecedented. The current storm is not unprecedented in duration or degree.

Whenever an editor sees a superlative, a red flag should go up in his or her mind. So after I read that script, I phoned the meteorologist in Kansas City and asked him about the weather the previous day, when the script was telecast. That's how I found out the correspondent was wrong. (See entries under *Accuracy* and *Learned.*)

"Twice-purged Chinese moderate Teng Hsiao-Ping is believed headed for an unprecedented second political comeback."

Yet another "unprecedented." Through casual overuse, the word has become meaningless. For whom is the comeback unprecedented? For Teng? For China? For the world? For the writer?

Yes, nowadays we spell his name "Deng Xiaoping." And he's no longer lo mein on the totem pole.

This is a more recent CBS News script:

"One bright note in the course of this tragedy has been the unprecedented cooperation between the U.S. and Ethiopia, two governments that haven't always been the best of friends."

Perhaps the writer means the cooperation was unprecedented for the United States and Ethiopia's current government. When he says they haven't always been the best of friends, some listeners might wonder, Were they ever?

"The time set for the execution of Utah killer Gary Gilmore is now less than 26 hours away . . . and attorneys seeking to protect other clients condemned to death are down to one final appeal. Today they will seek a stay order from Associate Justice Byron White of the U-S Supreme Court."

They were not "down to one final appeal"; they seemed to be. After White turned 'em down, they went to Blackmun, who also turned 'em down. Then they went to a Federal district judge in Salt Lake City, who did stay the execution.

Here's a recent broadcast example from a TV station:

"The sixth and final F-B-I report arrived at the White House today before it landed at the Capitol. The report is 140 pages long, but the White House says there's nothing in it that should prevent John Tower's nomination as defense secretary . . . ."

In fact, the F.B.I. report on Tower was not its last one on him. There were several more. Reminds me of the French actress Sarah Bernhardt, who came to this country for four Farewell Tours.

Nothing could prevent Tower's *nomination;* the President had already nominated him. The writer should have said *confirmation.*

A recent broadcast script from a radio station:

"The last word on Ted Bundy's execution comes from Bundy himself. In a taped interview before he went to Florida's electric chair, the serial killer said he deserved to die. . . ."

The last word on Bundy: We'll never know who's going to utter it—or when.

I'd also like to have a word with the person who wrote another script on the same subject at the same station:

"Convicted killer Ted Bundy . . singing like a bird, as his date with Old Sparky approaches. The 42-year-old law school dropout has confessed to. . . ."

In news stories about death, slang and sarcasm are in bad taste.

The script's first sentence lacks a tense. And lacks sense. The tense that reports an action occurring in the present, the present progressive tense, would be "is singing." It is effective in underlining the continuing nature of an action or an action that occurs repeatedly. But in the lead of that script, ''singing,'' a present participle, should be accompanied by a helping verb that's a form of *to be,* like *is. Singing,* standing alone, is a participle (which is an adjective, *not* a verb). Better: ''Convicted killer Ted Bundy *is singing* like a bird as his date. . . .''

Listeners might instantly regard the absence of *is* in the script as a sign that *singing like a bird* is to be followed by a verb. Maybe they'd expect something like this: ''Convicted killer Ted Bundy, singing like a bird, pleaded today to be let out of his cage.'' Instead, we tumble into a void. No verb.

When we write for the eye, we need to keep in mind readability, the quality of being readable. And when we write for the ear, we have to think about *listenability.* Does this script work for the listener? Writers may work for editors or producers, but scripts must work for listeners. Can listeners grasp the script the first time they hear it? They get only one crack at it, so the first time is also the last time.

A hint for newscasters who start a nightly Wall Street wrap-up by saying, ''Stock prices *going* up today'': English-speaking (and -listening) people not liking. *Going,* a participle, is *not* a verb. A finite verb—one with a tense—is more powerful than a batch of *-ing* words—gerunds and participles. It's stronger to say, ''Stock prices *went up* today.'' (See entry under *Ing*-lish.)

Consider the tense used in newspaper headlines and occasionally in newscasts, the historical present: ''Bundy Sings Like Bird as Fry Day Nears.'' We can understand that head easily. It has two verbs, *sings* and *nears.* Except for the odd tense and the lack of an *a* before *Bird,* we have a complete sentence. And we know what it means—without hesitation.

But the lead of the first Bundy script is an incomplete sentence. And a confusing one. Sometimes an incomplete sentence works, but the one in the script sounds like an immigrant's grappling with our strange language.

"Throughout the campaign, Tanaka insisted he is innocent and that the trial will vindicate him. The court proceedings, deliberately delayed until after the election, promise to be the most significant legal action of postwar Japan."

How about the trial of war criminals by the International Tribunal after WW II?

In that case, Japan's premier during World War Two, General Tojo, and six other leaders were sentenced to death and hanged.

"Maurice Douglass, a second-string defensive back for the Chicago Bears, got the word from the N-F-L this morning and left training camp, victim of the N-F-L's first-ever sanction against players for using anabolic steroids, the first time any professional athletes have been penalized for using strength-enhancing drugs."

First things first: This is a recent CBS News script.

The script's first *first* is justified. But the sentence is far too long (47 words), and the second *first* should be used in a second sentence.

What makes this script worthy of inclusion here is the use of *first-ever.* Whenever I hear *first-ever,* I wonder whether it's the first since the dawn of time.

Not only is *first-ever* redundant, it's a time-waster and a sign of overwriting, another twofer in the torrent of tawdry tautology tainting our tongue. If an event is the first, it's automatically the first *ever.* So there's no need for first-*ever,* most-*ever* and best-*ever.* Never, ever.

And since when is someone who's punished for violating a rule labeled a *victim*? Or is that another first?

Too many writers dote on "firsts." Occasionally, a "first" is of significance, but many that we read or hear about are trivial, improbable or unprovable.

Another absolute that's perilous is *only.* The Museum of Science and Industry in Chicago displays a U-boat captured by the U.S. Navy in World War Two. A plaque proclaims it "the only German submarine ever boarded and captured at sea."[6] And the wartime U.S. Chief of Naval Operations called the capture "the most unique and dramatic incident of the antisubmarine war in the Atlantic."[7] But a British historian later disclosed that the Royal Navy had boarded and captured a U-boat well before the U.S. Navy caught the U-505.[8] The British had kept their catch secret lest the enemy learn that their codes and a code machine had been taken. For security, even the Admiralty's records, except for one small file, showed the sub had been sunk. And another *only* has been blown out of the water.

---

6. The same assertion is made by Rear Admiral Daniel V. Gallery, USN, in his *We Captured a U-Boat* (London: Sidgwick and Jackson, 1957), 67.

7. Ernest J. King and Walter Muir Whitehill, *Fleet Admiral King: A Naval Record* (New York: W. W. Norton, 1952), 554. "Unique" means *one of a kind* and never takes a comparative or a superlative. So "most unique" is ungrammatical.

8. Stephen Roskill, *The Secret Capture* (London: Collins, 1959), 14.

A recent CBS News script:

"One of the nation's biggest, best known banks today was ordered to pay and agreed to pay the biggest-ever civil fine by the Treasury Department, a record four-and-three-quarter-million-dollar penalty to be paid by Bank of America. The government says it failed to report an estimated 17,000 cash transactions above $10,000. Federal officials cited no criminal activity by the bank itself, but said the Bank of America's failure to report large cash transactions almost certainly, quote, 'deprived the government of leads in drug, tax and other investigations,' unquote."

Besides *biggest-ever,* the script has several flaws:

The bank is one of the most *widely* known, not *best* known. If it had been the *best* known or even *well* known, the government might have known long ago what was going on.

If *today* is needed at all, it should be placed somewhere *after* the verb. *Today* is implicit in every story; it's better to tell a listener what happened than to take time for a word that's already taken for granted. Listeners assume today's newscasts are carrying today's news.

If the fine *was* the biggest, it had to be a record. So using *biggest* and *record* in the same sentence goes beyond what's justifiable. As long as the word *fine* has been used, there's no need to use *penalty* in the same sentence. And two *biggest*s and *pay, pay* and *paid* in one sentence are too much. Much too much.

In the second sentence, *it* seems to refer to the government. And in the third sentence, *itself* is unneeded.

Listeners can confuse *cited* with *sighted.* (See *Homophones.*)

No need for *quote* and *unquote.* Without those intrusive words, the quotation means the same, whether attributed or unattributed. (See *Quote/End Quote/Unquote.*)

Stronger: "One of the biggest banks, Bank of America, has been fined almost five million dollars. It's the largest civil fine ever imposed by the Treasury Department."

Truth is shorter than fiction. Or magnification.

Accuracy

"[Anchor]: The time grows short for the presidency of Gerald Ford, and today he took obvious pride and pleasure in presenting the Medal of Freedom to 22 American civilians to honor them for outstanding accomplishment. ________ ________ was there to report on the ceremony.

"[Reporter]: President Ford bent low to place the blue and white ribbon around the neck of the country's only living five-star General of the Army, Omar Bradley, who is in a wheelchair. . . ."

Five-star generals do fade away but not into civilian life. The lead-in could read: "22 Americans to honor. . . ."

"The President noted that three nominees to his cabinet—Griffin Bell to Justice, Joseph Califano to Health, Education and Welfare, and Raymond Marshall to Labor—have for various reasons not yet been given the required advice and consent of the Senate."

The Senate gives its advice and consent to the President, not to nominees. Better: ". . . not yet been *approved* by the Senate."

"Her former husband, Andy Williams, who was with her during the trial, was with her again for the sentencing, which may be appealed."

One doesn't appeal a trial or a sentencing; one can appeal a conviction and, in a few states, a sentence.

Adverbs

"Boats literally cannot move; from Cairo to Saint Louis, 38 barges and 300 tows literally locked in the ice."

If the boats can't move, they can't move. "Literally" adds nothing but length.

"Literally" twice in one sentence! That's twice as bad.

My memo to the writer of that script didn't take. Or else he suffered a relapse. Nine years later, in 1986, he wrote:

"Using a network of computers and one-million U-S tax dollars, 37-hundred [family planning] centers dot the countryside, dispensing information and literally tons of birth control devices."

And on the same newscast, the anchor said:

"Ted Bundy is a law school dropout convicted of killing three young women and suspected of killing literally dozens of others."

"I would never use *literally* in a million years," René J. Cappon says in *The Word: An Associated Press Guide to Good Writing*; "I mean that figuratively." He says *literally* is "disastrous as a casual intensifier because it means that something is factually and precisely true. *The Mets literally slaughtered the Cardinals last night* would have left at least nine corpses."

Another guide says of *literally*: "As generally used, the adverb *literally,* like *actually,* doesn't mean much. It merely adds emphasis, often to a statement that doesn't need it. *Literally* should mean 'in the strict sense' or 'without exaggeration,' but it usually means quite the opposite—'figuratively.' Sentences like 'I literally died laughing' or 'I was literally walking on air' obviously shouldn't be taken at face value. If *literally* always were used precisely, it could have considerable force, showing that a seeming hyperbolic or figurative statement is a matter of fact: 'Her voice could literally shatter glass'; 'He can't come to the phone,' Houdini's secretary said, 'He's literally tied up.' Try to keep *literally* out of your writing unless you mean it literally. Abuses of the word can seem ludicrous, and those who recognize them enjoy pointing them out."[9] Among those who point them out is the *New York Times*'s in-house monitor, *Winners & Sinners*:

---

9. Claire Kehrwald Cook, *Line by Line: How to Edit Your Own Writing* (Boston: Houghton Mifflin, 1985), 185.

''By far the most common feature of jazzed-up writing is the unnecessary use of adverbs. We get 'sharply' and 'flatly,' 'squarely' and 'roundly,' the most ubiquitous of all . . . 'bitterly.' By haphazard count, at least 9 out of 10 of these adverbs are superfluous.

''If someone is denounced, what is added to the meaning by saying he was 'bitterly denounced'? If someone is rebuked, what is gained by saying he was 'sharply rebuked'?

''If something is denied, isn't it just as 'denied' as it would be if it were 'flatly denied'?''

Undeniably, correct pronunciation is important, so let's look at—or listen to—some odd ways of pronouncing place names. Cairo, the locale of that script, is pronounced KAY-roe. It's one of many U.S. cities pronounced differently from foreign cities with the same names. Vienna, Illinois, for example, is pronounced VIE-enna, and Marseilles, Illinois, is pronounced Mar-SAYLES. In Louisiana, the town of Natchitoches is pronounced NAK-uh-tish. And in Ohio, Bellefontaine is pronounced Bell-fountain. And some names are pronounced differently in other states. So a newscaster who moves to another locale should familiarize himself with localisms.

"Still, it's only certain kinds of cars that are selling: Sales of the big Pontiacs are way up, and Oldsmobile actually is reporting a record in sales for this time of year."

Actually is unnecessary. The sentence means the same without it. *Really.*

Here's a sentence that's far too long, 56 words:

"The major opponents are such liberal groups as the Americans for Democratic Action, the Congressional Black Caucus and the N-A-A-C-P, which has filed a statement with the Judiciary Committee asking that the nomination be shelved until after Mr. Carter is actually sworn in, in order to give opponents more time to look into Judge Bell's past."

"Actually" is extraneous.

Adverbs tend to be superfluous. And they often express a point of view. We stay neutral in a story, but adverbs can slant it. Newswriters should skip *absolutely, actually, awfully, candidly, frankly, honestly, fortunately, unfortunately, incredibly, gradually, grimly, suddenly, eventually, finally, ultimately, inevitably, ironically, luckily, miraculously, naturally, obviously, perfectly, personally, positively, practically, really, sadly, seriously, successfully, totally, undoubtedly, unquestionably, virtually, basically, completely, essentially, fittingly, specifically* and most other adverbs. Usually.

As for *arguably,* a synonym for *debatably* or *questionably,* and *firstly, secondly, lastly, importantly* and *indisputably*: neverly.

The use of *ironically* reminds me of how often writers inject *ironic, ironically* or *irony* in their copy—when the story has no irony at all. A recent CBS example:

"Talk about ironies. Twenty years ago, the Jefferson Airplane liked to joke that if they ever hit middle age, they'd call themselves the Jefferson Wheelchair. Now they're gearing up to tour."

Irony, according to a dictionary, is "a method of humorous or subtly sarcastic expression in which the intended meaning of the words used is the direct opposite of their usual sense." Also: "a combination of circumstances or a result that is the opposite of what is or might be expected or considered appropriate."

So where is that story's irony?

Another adverb to avoid: *incidentally.* Some newscasters use it to preface a tag or button. But if something *is* incidental, it probably shouldn't be used on air at all. And if it's consequential, it shouldn't be diminished with *incidentally.*

Another cavil in this cavil-cade: Whenever I hear an item like this, I wonder about it: "*Incidentally,* the President is going to spend the weekend at Camp David." Does the anchor mean the visit is incidental to the newscast or to the President?

Definitely is another adverb to avoid. If you're overpowered by an urge to use *definitely,* recall this observation by a British humorist: "I offer a prize to the first foreman of a jury to announce a verdict of *definitely guilty* and another to the judge who informs the prisoner that he will be 'definitely hanged until he is very definitely dead.' "[10]

Whatever the world might need, it does not need new adverbs. But a CBS News anchor recently hatched a doozy:

"Overnight, the torrential winds and the rains of Hurricane Hugo bear [*bear?*] down very <u>bruntly</u> on the southeast coastline and hit Charleston very, very hard. . . ."

10. Sir Ernest Gowers, *The Complete Plain Words* (Baltimore: Penguin Books, 1954), 88. The author is quoting Sir Alan Herbert.

The anchor went on to call it a "very breaking" story. *"Very* breaking"? "Very *bruntly*"? Verily, I say unto you: speak English! (Was the anchor thinking of that old NBC News team, Bruntly and Hinkley?)

Very is also used there as an adverb. Misused. And overused, frequently as an intensifier to mean *extremely* or *absolutely.* Rather than sprinkle scripts with *very,* it's better to choose the right words. Instead of saying someone is *very* tired, for example, you can say she's *exhausted.* Or instead of *"very* large," try *huge.*

Write with nouns and verbs, Strunk and White remind us, not with adjectives and adverbs.[11] The authors tell us to avoid qualifiers—*little, pretty, rather, very.* "These are the leeches," they say, "that infest the pond of prose, sucking the blood of words."[12]

"His recall for consultations was an act of diplomatic protest several steps short of an actual break in relations."

"Actual" adds nothing, except time.

Actual is an adjective, not an adverb, but the waste of time is the same.

"Selick also discussed the actual breakup, which he claims followed collision with a 40-foot wall of water."

---

11. William Strunk Jr. and E. B. White, *The Elements of Style,* 3d ed. (New York: Macmillan, 1979), 71.

12. *The Elements of Style,* 73.

An "actual" breakup is the same as a breakup.

Collision with a wall of water? In this case, the "wall of water" was an ocean wave. When two ships run into each other, it's a collision. When a ship and a wave meet, we usually speak of a ship's slamming into a wave, or a wave's slamming, striking or pounding a ship. Or of waves hammering, crashing into, or sweeping across a ship. But *colliding*?

Advise/Inform

"The Utah state medical examiner says Gary Gilmore lived for two minutes after a prison firing squad shot him. The doctor said he could not say whether the condemned man suffered during that time, but he did advise that shock usually sets in with the impact, impeding pain. The medical examiner conducted a three-hour autopsy on Gilmore's remains. He said all four bullets struck within an inch or two of each other near Gilmore's heart."

Advise = give advice. "Advise" is not synonymous with "inform."

Rather than "of each other," the line should read "of one another." "Each other" is used with two persons or units; "one another" is used with three or more.

I hope it's not too late: *advise* is a transitive verb, so it needs an object. You advise or inform *someone.* Instead of *advise,* the correspondent could have used *say.*

Instead of *remains,* make it *body.* Better: "The medical examiner performed an autopsy that ran three hours."

No need for *on Gilmore's remains.* What else would the m.e. have been autopsying? The script?

Age

"Clifford Alexander, 43, a Washington lawyer, will be Secretary of the Army."

Broadcast style calls for ages to be used before names or identification, such as "43-year-old Clifford Alexander." Another acceptable way is "Clifford Alexander, who is 43 years old." The latter seems preferable because his age is not more important than his name. Still another way: "Actor Freddie Prinze is dead—at 22."

On second look, I'd make that "at the age of 22." Writing "Clifford Alexander, 43. . . ." is print style. For an unknown or an unfamiliar person, broadcasters put title or description before name: "A Washington lawyer, Clifford Alexander, has been chosen Secretary of the Army."

Stronger: "A new Secretary of the Army has been appointed: a Washington lawyer, Clifford Alexander." It's stronger because it builds up to the key word or words: the name of the appointee and his identification. As the sentence rolls on, it builds suspense and retains a listener's interest to the end. So I'd write a story about most other appointments and awards in the same way: "The American League's Most Valuable Player title was awarded today to the Chicago White Sox first baseman, Eddie Spageddi." And "The Nobel Peace Prize was awarded today to Tibet's exiled leader, the Dalai Lama."

Everyone has an age, so I wouldn't lead a story with an age, such as ''43-year-old Clifford Alexander.'' But if the story were about a boy, for instance, I might write, ''A 12-year-old boy from Boston broke the bank at Monte Carlo.'' And if you write about a boy or girl, you needn't call him or her ''young.'' There are no old boys or girls, except in those social networks.

In most broadcast stories, age is unnecessary. If age is relevant, I might give the age a sentence of its own: ''The new justice of the U-S Supreme Court is 30 years old.'' I would not refer to him as ''the 30-year-old Johnson,'' as though he were an object, like a 30-year-old couch, instead of someone on the bench.

This local script is typical of too many we hear—and probably many we don't hear:

"A 38-year-old man is on his way to the Grady Burn Unit following a chemical spill in East Atlanta. Vernon Woodall is in stable condition with burns over 15 percent of his body. Atlanta police are not sure what caused the spill of the chemical, phenol, a class B poison."

The first thing a listener hears is an age, which may be the least important and least interesting fact in the story. And the age delays arrival at what the story is all about. Stronger: ''A chemical spill in an East Atlanta factory has left a worker badly burned.''

''There seems to be a universal law—at least among newsmen—that the age of every person mentioned in a story must be supplied,'' according to the *UPI Broadcast Stylebook*. ''Nonsense,'' it says: ''Use age only when it has a direct bearing on the story. There is little point in giving the age of a woman whose pet cat found its way home after being given to a nephew who lives 186 miles away.''

Cub reporters are obsessed with getting every subject's age. Name, age, address and occupation. They pursue those facts because editors drum that drill (drum a *drill*?) into their heads. Reminds me of a shaggy bear story: A bear in a Chicago zoo tore off a man's arm. And a police reporter, trying to meet a deadline, managed to ferret out a few fast facts. He phoned the city desk and was transferred to a rewrite man. The rewrite man hurriedly took the fragments and whipped out a good story, just in time to make the first edition. When the top editor, a former colonel, read the dupes, he charged into the city room and—without even a salute to the speedy rewriter—demanded, ''How *old* was the bear?''

Agreement of Subject and Verb

"There is still lots of snow, lots of road to clear, lots of homes and businesses to shovel out. But the nightmare is over. At least, everyone in this storm-battered city <u>hope</u> it is. Buffalo is slowly coming back to life. Stores are re-opening. Buses and trains are running again, and there'll be even more vehicles on the roads today, now that the travel ban has been lifted. A state of emergency is still technically in effect, but it may not be for long, especially if the weather holds and snow removal crews can keep working. Many major thoroughfares already have been cleared, but many more need to be. Damage from the storm has been estimated at 60-million dollars."

Everyone hopes.

Subject and verb must agree.

Before we shovel off to Buffalo, I should point out that the anchor led into this correspondent's report by identifying the city and state, so the correspondent was able to defer mention of the city. But his lead is weak. "There is" is a dead phrase, so it's best to avoid it. (See *There Is/There Are.*)

Better: "Buffalo's nightmare seems almost over. The city still has to clear snow from many miles of roads, and people have to shovel out tens of thousands of homes and businesses. But Buffalo is slowly returning to life."

As for "lots" and "lot," *Composition and Rhetoric,* a high school textbook, says, 'Both words are vulgarly used in the sentence, 'He has a lot of money and lots of friends.' The book was published in 1908. Since then, language has changed a lot. "A lot of" has become acceptable in serious writing, but the *Oxford Guide to English Usage* (1983) says "lots of" is not acceptable. Another problem with "lots of": it's vague. Instead of "lots of," try "much," "many," or something closer to the exact number.

A recent CBS News script:

"We live in an age of celebrity in which it seems everyone wants their picture taken. . . ."

Everyone, anyone, someone and *no one* take the singular. Correct: "everyone wants his picture taken." But if the writer wanted to skirt the masculine, he could have changed everyone to people everywhere.''

"Blumenthal—along with other top administration economic advisers—are to appear before the House Appropriations Committee."

Make it "is."

Subjects and verbs should agree even when misleading words or phrases come between them. Usually these intervening words are prepositional phrases like "in addition to," "as well as" and "together with," and they don't affect the number of the subject.

"The Soviet Foreign Ministry said today an American couple has been granted political asylum. Apparently, they hadn't been too successful in the United States."

This CBS News script points up another problem with agreement. The script tried to have it both ways, first using a singular verb with *couple,* then a plural pronoun. When *couple* refers to two persons, it takes a plural verb. Exception: "Each couple was asked to bring a gift for the grab bag." When you're tempted to write "the couple *is,*" think about this: "The couple is going on *its* honeymoon." Correct: "The couple *are* going on *their* honeymoon."

P.S. When *couple* is used to mean *a few,* it's followed by *of.*

"Neither President Reagan nor his aides seems to have known much about what was going on aboard."

This CBS News script presents a different problem with agreement—or disagreement. The verb should be governed by the last noun, *aides*. That would make it *seem*. The rule: When the subjects differ in number, the verb agrees with the nearest subject.

A leading expert on our language, Theodore M. Bernstein, says disagreement in number between subject and verb is the most persistently recurring error in news writing—and perhaps in other writing as well. These errors, he says, "arise out of haste and carelessness, out of failure to look back to see what the actual subject of the verb is. They are bad enough when committed by the writer, but they are unpardonable when passed by the copy editor."[13]

"Using it even once can make a person crave cocaine for as long as they live."

This recent example comes from ABC News. Perhaps the anchor was striving to be non-sexist, so instead of saying "as long as *he* lives," he tried to tiptoe around the minefield. But with *they*, he put his foot in it. He could have sidestepped the problem by saying, "People who use cocaine, even once, can crave it for as long as they live." The key word is *can*. I assume it means that not everyone who uses cocaine will crave it for life, but it *can* happen. If that is true, it would be stronger to say, "Anyone who uses co-

13. Theodore M. Bernstein, *More Language That Needs Watching* (Manhasset, N.Y.: Channel Press, 1962), 21.

caine, even once, can crave it as long as he lives.'' For me, *he* applies to all humankind. But if that *he* bothers you, write, ''Anyone who uses cocaine, even once, can crave it for life.''

Another example from ABC News:

"Each state has their own laws, and parents facing this type of dilemma have to study the laws. Also, in many states, they disconnect irregardless of the law. In fact, in the Chicago, Illinois, area, we found hospitals that said . . . ."

Each takes the singular, so the correspondent should have said, ''Each state has *its* own laws.''

Major cities, and Chicago is still one of them, don't need to be accompanied by their states.

Irregardless? Whether he meant *irrespective* or *regardless,* the non-word *irregardless* is an illiteracy.

All That

"It's designed to be shot into space, orbit the planet and land back on earth like an airplane. But first they had to get the space shuttle from the factory to the testing site. So at dawn this morning, they simply hitched up a trailer and hauled it down the road. Well, it wasn't all that simple."

If the phrase is needed, "all that" should be changed to "at all." But the sentence reads just as well without any such locution.

What I tried to say but didn't quite, was: the writer could have said, "Well, it wasn't simple *at all.*"

During the *Second Look* project, I also squirreled away the next two scripts:

"McDermitt is sort of interesting, too . . . but didn't do all that well in school. . . ."

" . . . the idea being, of course, that it can't be all that cold."

I never got around to writing to those writers and telling them why the underlined words need replacement. In both passages, *all that* implies a comparison that's never made. In the first script, the writer could have written, "didn't do well." Or "didn't do well at all." Or "didn't do especially well." Or "did poorly." The second script could also have been sharpened.

"All that," a Briticism, sounds affected in this country, according to a usage expert, Roy H. Copperud, who says most usage experts oppose it.[14] Theodore M. Bernstein says it's best avoided because it's "not all that good."[15]

---

14. Roy H. Copperud, *American Usage and Style* (New York: Van Nostrand Reinhold, 1980), 17.

15. Theodore M. Bernstein, *Dos, Don'ts and Maybes of English Usage* (New York: Times Books, 1977), 13.

Anxious/Eager

"Probably nobody is more anxious to come to Washington and see the inauguration today than the people in Mr. Carter's home town, Plains, Georgia."

In this sense, please use "eager." "Anxious" carries worry and uneasiness.

As Expected

"As expected, President Ford has asked Congress for a ten-billion-dollar cut in individual income taxes. . . . The overall tax plan is practically a carbon copy of one rejected by Congress last year. . . ."

"As expected" makes whatever follows less newsy. Chances are, most of our listeners weren't expecting that news. I know I wasn't.

Whenever I hear "as expected," I wonder who's expectant (or who's the expector).

News is what's new. Or it's something that has changed. *As expected* or *as predicted* at the top takes the edge off the story. Imagine this lead: "As expected, George Bush was sworn in today as President. And, as predicted, he chose Millie as First Dog."

As you might not have expected, a more recent CBS News script illustrates even better what's wrong with *as expected*:

"In Washington, the Republican-controlled Senate, as expected, voted overwhelmingly today to ban President Reagan's proposed massive arms sale until next March, unless Jordan and Israel begin direct peace talks."

For openers, where else would the Senate meet *but* Washington?

As for *as expected,* how many listeners could have been expecting the Senate to vote overwhelmingly to ban the arms sale until March? I didn't even know the Senate was in session.

A local station (ever hear of a *national* station?):

"As expected, Mayor Washington made public his 2-point-7-billion-dollar budget proposal for 1988. And as expected, it was met with stinging attacks from City Council critics."

City Hall reporters were expecting the budget. And some other people, too: editors, public officials and payrollers. But the general populace? Relatively few. Even if the multitudes *were* expecting the mayor to release his budget, *as expected* is a poor way to start. And the problem is compounded by the second straight *as expected.*

Stronger: "Mayor Washington's budget for next year calls for spending more than two-and-a-half billion dollars." Or "Mayor Washington made public next year's budget today, and it calls for spending more than two-and-a-half billion dollars."

Attribution

"The most important witness in the Claudine Longet manslaughter case will be Miss Longet herself. That's according to defense attorney Charles Weedman, who says Longet will appear among a host of witnesses so the defense can show that she and her boyfriend, Spider Sabich, were getting along well at the time he was shot."

The newscaster shouldn't start by calling someone "the most important witness." A casual listener would assume that the newscaster was making that judgment. There's no way such an evaluation could be made until after everyone testifies. Even then, the jurors themselves are probably the best judges. And it's doubtful they'd draw up a list of the "Ten Most Important Witnesses." Alternatives: "Singer Claudine Longet is going to take the stand, and her lawyer says she'll be the most important witness in her manslaughter trial. . . ." Or: "The lawyer for singer Claudine Longet says she'll be the most important witness in her manslaughter trial. Attorney Charles Weedman says she'll be one of many defense witnesses who'll testify that. . . ."

The pattern of leading a script with a debatable or startling statement, or any statement at all, and then following it with "That's according to. . . ." or "So says" is not conversational. And it's not broadcast style. Neither is accepted by experts in broadcast newswriting. CBS's own book on television news reporting presents the rule forcefully:

"When writing for television, always say *who* before you say *what* someone said or did. . . . The viewer is entitled to know the authority for a statement or action first so that he can gauge what importance to attach to it as the newscaster relates it. . . . Do not make the mistake of leading a story with an interesting quote and then identifying the speaker in the second sentence. Almost inevitably, some viewers will miss the connection and will accept the quote as the newscaster's own opinion.''[16]

In *Broadcast Newswriting,* Tim Wulfemeyer says, ''We ALWAYS report attribution at the beginning of a sentence, because that's the way we report it in our everyday conversations.''[17]

In sum: Attribution before assertion. That rule applies whether you're writing for radio or TV, AM or FM, VHF or UHF, A.M. or P.M.

"Soldiers from the United Arab Emirates are moving into positions in southern Lebanon tonight, according to reports reaching Beirut."

Broadcast style calls for placing attribution at the beginning of a sentence. Sometimes, it's O.K. to place attribution in the middle, but not at the end.

I should have explained what I meant by ''middle.'' For example: ''The best way to proceed,'' Senator Smith says, ''is to turn the problem over to the states.''

"According to an opinion poll published today in Glasgow, about one Scot in three does not favor self-government, despite plans to hold a referendum on the

16. The Staff of CBS News, *Television News Reporting* (New York: McGraw-Hill, 1958), 119.

17. K. Tim Wulfemeyer, *Broadcast Newswriting* (Ames, Iowa: Iowa State University Press, 1983), 15.

subject. Conservative opponents of more self-rule say it will also mean more taxes, more politicians and more over-government."

Instead of starting out with "according to," how about making it: "An opinion poll published in Glagow today says one Scot. . . ." I don't know which other stories were available at that hour [1 p.m.], but as for this item, I would have scotched it.

In my haste, I dropped the "s" from Glasgow. And, also, I should have knocked "out" from "starting out."

Now that I have that off my chest, let's consider "according to." Those are dull words. Avoid starting a story with them, unless you want to alert listeners that the story they're about to hear is unconfirmed or unconfirmable.

The lead is out of kilter (semi-pun intended): Excluding those who are undecided (whatever their number), most people probably favor more self-rule. The *despite* suggests those who oppose self-government are doing so almost in defiance of the referendum.

But who cares?

Awkward Expression

"A swimmer had his medal taken away because he had been given an illegal medication, the doctor's fault."

I doubt that the swimmer engineered the removal of his medal, yet that's what the "had" makes it read. When I hear someone say so-and-so "had his leg broken," I half-expect him to add, "to collect insurance." This can be fixed by saying, "A swimmer's medal was taken away because. . . ."

"State offices in Minnesota have been directed to cut back on operations to save energy. Similar steps are being taken in the Dayton, Ohio, area, where 24 counties have been declared in a state of emergency because of dwindling supplies of natural gas."

Awkward. Better: "Similar steps are being taken in Dayton, Ohio, and surrounding counties. And because of dwindling supplies of natural gas, Ohio's governor has declared a state of emergency in that area."

After you read the original script, you may wonder why Minnesota is short of energy. And why is one section of Ohio short of natural gas?

Newswriters need to ask themselves *why*? Even if we don't use the answers in our script, we must constantly ask *why* for guidance in our writing.

"The cold wave has been so bitter here that some 300 companies that use natural gas have had their supplies cut off so that residential customers can stay warm."

That sounds as though the 300 companies called for the cut-off.

"Bearded residents of Argentina are being faced with a difficult decision. They must either shave their bushy chins—or become outlaws. The Argentine government has decreed that from now on all male residents must be clean shaven for the pictures which appear on their identity cards . . ."

Make it "are facing."

Better yet: "Bearded residents of Argentina face a difficult decision." (Please don't call my revision face-saving.)

Is the decision difficult? Is shaving backbreaking? In fact, as the script tells us, men need be clean shaven only for their I.D. cards; it does not say they have to be clean shaven at any other time. What's the big deal? Who cares? And why is it news in *our* country? Because the wire services moved it? Just because it moves, you don't need to salute it.

"President Reagan tonight is quoted to CBS News as saying, 'I was terribly impressed by this Russian fellow.' End quote."

Is quoted to doesn't sound like English. (See *Quote/ End Quote/Unquote.*)

"President Carter mixed his concern today for the increasing problems caused by the cold weather with a handful of foreign policy topics."

Looks like a mixaphor.

"Mixaphor" is a word used by Theodore M. Bernstein to describe a mixed metaphor. The script, which opened the newscast, said Jimmy Carter *mixed his concern* with a *handful* of topics. The writer tried to combine the two top stories: the cold and foreign policy. Usually, such combos don't dovetail and for good reason: They are not related.

Bad/Badly

"Do you feel badly about the breakup of Lib's marriage?"

What the CBS News anchor should have said is *bad*. *Badly* means *incorrectly, harmfully,* or *wickedly.*

Verbs of sense (*feel, smell, taste*) take adjectives as complements, not adverbs. So we'd say, "The milk tastes bad." The only time to use an adverb after *feel* is when the adverb modifies the verb rather than the subject: "I feel strongly about that." And an inept student of Braille could say, correctly, "I feel badly."

As Clifton Fadiman once observed: "Don't feel bad when you hear the broadcaster say he feels badly. Just remember that all men are created equally."[18]

Bad Taste

"For at least one Liberian tanker captain—'Here come de judge' . . ."

It's an arresting lead, but I wouldn't be Flip about an ecological disaster (in dialect yet, besides).

---

18. William and Mary Morris, *Harper Dictionary of Contemporary Usage*, 2d ed. (New York: Harper & Row, 1985), 61.

"Here come de judge" was a catch phrase made popular by the comedian Flip Wilson. We don't have fun with disasters—ecological or lexicological—and we don't deliver news in dialect.

"A Chicago judge has come up with a gift for the man who has everything: a four-year prison term. The recipient of the gift is Robert Ferguson, who comes from a family of multi-millionaires. The sentence was following Ferguson's conviction on charges of swindling a Miami bank out of nearly 1 million dollars."

We don't make fun of someone who's put behind bars. The script, reprinted here in full, doesn't say the man himself has everything, or even *any*thing. His coming from a rich family doesn't mean he's rich. Or even solvent.

The last sentence of the script says Ferguson's sentence "was following." Should be "followed."

Beings

"Human beings also can risk cancer. . . ."

Strike "beings." "Humans" does the job.

Bitter

". . . The bitter cold eased up in most of the East today. . . ."

". . .The bitter weather has caused a surge in unemployment. . . ."

". . .It was 25 degrees below zero at the time, with bitter winds. . . ."

". . .But there is a shortage of readily available supplies, and there is, as with the oil embargo, a bitter argument over its causes. . . ."

"And in Buffalo, Police Captain Henry Pauley says thieves are taking advantage of the harsh winter."

Congratulations! I've been reading so much about bitter cold, bitter weather, bitter winds, bitter controversies, bitter arguments, etc., that I was pleased to find another (and entirely apt) adjective.

The writer: David Jackson.

It's to my regret—though not bitter regret—that I commented only on the last script in this section during the short life of *Second Look*. What I would have said, and what I shall say now, is that *bitter* is overused by newswriters almost as much as *major*: bitter attack, bitter battle, bitter controversy, bitter debate, bitter defeat, bitter dispute, bitter enemy, bitter exchange, bitter experience, bitter memory, bitter opposition, bitter pill, bitter end. "Bitter" is a good word, and so are the other 200,000 words in a desk dictionary, but too much of even a good thing leaves a bitter taste.

If "bitter" keeps popping into your head when you write, consult a word doctor, in particular, Dr. Peter Roget. He created the *Thesaurus of English Words and Phrases, Classified and Arranged so as to Facilitate the Expression of Ideas and Assist in Literary Composition.* It's even more valuable today than when first published in 1852. This storehouse of synonyms has been revised several times and is now in its fourth edition. If you don't have it in your library, make it your next addition. And use it. That is an order—command, mandate, injunction.

Blaze

"A fire that raged through the small New York State town of Philmont last night is now reported contained. The only hot spot remaining—inside the manufacturing plant where it's believed to have started. Before firefighters could get a handle on the blaze, half the buildings in the village were burned down. The entire population—17-hundred people—had to be evacuated. No serious injuries reported."

I've seen firemen put a handpump on a fire, but I can't visualize their getting a handle on one.

I should have taken time to say more about that script, so I'll take it now:

That second sentence is terrible. I can't fix it, though, because I don't know what it means.

A blaze is not a full-blown fire; it's what you have when your wastebasket is on fire.

A manufacturing plant = factory.

A village ranks in size between a hamlet and a town, and they're exceeded in size by a city. Good writers apply those labels with care.

When the script says half the buildings *were* burned down, it suggests arson. Let's say only that they *burned down.*

The entire population *had* to be evacuated? They *were* evacuated, but it's possible they didn't have to be.

Buried Lead

"The Panamanian vessel Crown Pearl, with a crew of 215 aboard, is heading for Midway Island in the Pacific. It's been taking on water. . . ."

That a ship is heading for Midway is not newsworthy. Unless you mention distress in the first sentence, the lead is ho-hum. Dump "aboard."

The script is burdened with what's known in the trade as a buried lead.

Characterizing News

"The Soviet Union seldom reports crime or disaster, but there was an interesting exception today. . . ."

Let the listener decide whether it's interesting.

The way to make a story interesting is by writing it in a way that engages listeners' interest—not by describing a story as interesting.

Good newswriters don't characterize news as good. Or bad. They let listeners decide for themselves. What's bad news for one listener may be good news for another. But I doubt that any listeners sit around with clipboards checking off each story: "That one's good for me. This one is bad. And this next one is 'indeterminate.' " Nor do good writers habitually call stories *amazing, astounding, disturbing, dramatic, exciting, shocking or stunning.*

A recent script from CBS News:

"To tell you again the bad news of this evening, a United Airlines DC-10, attempting an emergency landing after it experienced hydraulic failure, crashed and cartwheeled and burned and broke apart just short of the runway at the Sioux City, Iowa, airport."

All by myself, I was able to figure out that the news was bad.

Better: "Repeating the top story: A United Airlines DC-10 tried to make an emergency landing at Sioux City, Iowa, crashed just short of a runway, cartwheeled, burned and broke apart."

Clichés

"Secretary of State Kissinger began his last full week in office yesterday with what is taken as his <u>swan song</u>."

This is the season for Washington officials to say goodby, so we should declare open season on swans and their songs (except Gloria Swansong). "Swan song" is a cliché, and it should be nipped in the nest. (Ever hear a swan sing?)

The *Encyclopædia Britannica* says the song of the dying swan is a myth. And experts say the swan does not sing, ever.

Some bird-lovers, though, argue that a swan's call *is* a song.

We're all capable of committing clichés, but it's best not to commit them to paper. The following examples come from a flock of CBS News writers. (Or is the collective noun *clutch, gaggle,* or a *babble* of writers?)

"The Senate Commerce Committee opened hearings on spills today, and Senator Russell Long and Transportation Secretary William Coleman locked horns. . . ."

"Lock horns" is a cliché.

Please allow only elk or moose to lock horns.

A man who spent a lifetime studying words, Eric Partridge, defined *cliché* as "an outworn commonplace; a phrase, or short sentence, that has become so hackneyed that careful speakers and scrupulous writers shrink from it because they feel that its use is an insult to the intelligence of their audience or public. . . ."[19] Not only is a cliché often uneconomical, Partridge says, but it's almost always unnecessary.

---

19. Eric Partridge, *A Dictionary of Clichés* (New York: E. P. Dutton & Co., 1963), 2.

"After six days of hearings and 33 witnesses, the Senate Judiciary Committee met late on Inauguration Eve to bite the bullet on Jimmy Carter's most controversial nominee."

"Bite the bullet" is a cliché, heavily gnawed.

"Surprised officials went into a series of closed-door meetings. . . ."

"Closed-door" is a cliché. I don't expect government officials to confer in an amphitheater.

"Life here has not been a bed of roses for them, but they're hanging in there."

Overuse has soiled even "a bed of neuroses." "Bed of roses" might have been vivid when it was first used, but now it's withered.

Another cliché: *hanging in there.*

"On too many occasions here, Mr. Carter's press officers have been left with needless egg on their faces."

"Egg on the face" is a shell-shocked veteran deserving retirement.

Don't splatter eggs on people's faces, unless you fling an omelet. And don't scramble your metaphors.

The script mentions "*needless* egg on their faces." Is it ever needed?

"President-elect Carter had his first taste of being in Washington, D-C's limelight at an inauguration eve performance by Hollywood and Broadway stars."

Curtis MacDougall's Interpretative Reporting called "in the limelight" a cliché 40 years ago. The fly in the ointment is that clichés no longer evoke instant imagery, except of a weary writer. It's not true that one cliché is worth 10,000 pictures.

Today, that cliché is even older.

A limelight is a stage light, so if *anyone* was in the limelight or center stage, it was the stars.

"President-elect Carter is heading back to Georgia after a day in Washington spent huddled with the leaders of the military establishment."

"Huddled" is a cliché. It deserves a long time-out or a trip to the showers.

If Jimmy Carter had done as much huddling as newscasters reported, by now he'd be round-shouldered.

The last word of the script, "establishment," is unnecessary.

"The Daoud case appears to be a textbook example of a maverick intelligence agency deliberately contravening the policies of its government."

"Textbook example" is a cliché.

"Contravene" is not a "broadcast word," one instantly understood by most listeners, one that's used in everyday conversation. Synonym: *violate.*

"As Mrs. Harris was garnering bouquets and brickbats before Senate Banking, Juanita Kreps was telling Senate Commerce what she will do if she gets to be Secretary of Commerce."

Cliché.

At least my memos were short-winded.

As you know, *as* can have several meanings, including *when, while* and *because.* Listeners may be confused as to which meaning that writer intended. The meaning of *as* determines which way the path will go. As writers, we shouldn't mislead listeners with tangled paths or a fork in the path. Rather, we should point the way clearly, keep listeners moving along briskly, and make sure they don't hesitate, stumble or drop out.

"Still, Proxmire says that Mrs. Harris's nomination is a leadpipe cinch."

"Leadpipe cinch" is a cliché. Even more of a cinch is an airtight, brassbound, copper-riveted cinch, but "cinch" alone will do the job. Cinch = sure thing.

That can often be deleted from copy with no loss in meaning, particularly after *says,* certainly that *that.*

"There won't be the usual shopping list that a President wants from Congress. . . ."

Please avoid "shopping list," "laundry list" and other shopworn phrases.

"In the aftermath of a chain of tanker mishaps, the Coast Guard has apparently invested in an ounce of prevention."

"In the aftermath of" is a cliché; so is "in the wake of." They're wordy ways to say "after" or "following." As for "mishap," it's hardly more than bad luck with slight consequences, so "mishap" is inappropriate for an environmental disaster.

"An ounce of prevention" sounds like a cliché that needs an ounce of curare.

"Egypt wrestles with riot aftermath."

"Wrestling" with an "aftermath"?

First student: "What's aftermath?" Second student: "Algebra."

"The Senate works late—wrestling with the Carter emergency energy plan."

Is all that wrestling necessary?

After I sent a memo to a writer for using "in the wake of," I received this memo, apparently from a deskmate:

"While I think all can agree that 'in the wake of . . .' is an overused phrase which perhaps should be avoided because of that, to say that it is equivalent to and should be replaced by after reflects an apparent lack of understanding of what a wake is. The dictionary defines a wake as "the track left by a vessel in the water," and says in the wake of refers to being in "the track of and usually keeping close to. . . ." As most people know from experience, the water in a wake has a certain kind of turbulence that can be hazardous to small vessels. The point here is that "in the wake of" as used by ________ reflects the unsettled conditions that prevailed in the country during and after the Vietnam War and Watergate, whereas a simple after would have no such meaning."

I sent this reply:

"Thanks for taking time to send me your thoughts about 'in the wake of.' Although I don't know what's going on in any other writer's mind (and sometimes not even in my own), I doubt that most writers are thinking of turbulence when they use "in the wake of." I'm sorry if my previous memo 'reflects an apparent lack of understanding of what a wake is.' I surely hope I do understand, considering all the wakes I've sailed in, washed my clothes in, left and attended.''

"The [Dow Industrial] average has broken through the magic barrier again and now stands at 1002.16."

"Magic barrier" and "magic number" are clichés. Besides, there's nothing magical about any point on the Dow.

The Dow may have psychological barriers or resistance levels, and some investors may seem to have a magical touch. I'd leave magic to Merlin.

"There is no smoking gun in Judge Bell's background, Henry said—no devastating incident that would obviously disqualify him."

"Smoking gun" was apt when applied to a certain unindicted co-conspirator, but now it's a burned-out cliché.

If it was burned out in 1977, by now it's reduced to dust.

''Most inferior writing is cliché-ridden,'' according to Roy H. Copperud, ''but journalese has developed its own clichés.'' The usage expert says: ''In journalese, a thing is not *kept secret,* but *a lid of secrecy* is clamped on it; rain and snow do not *fall,* but *are dumped*; rivers do not *overflow* or *flood,* but *go on a rampage*; honors are not *won* or *earned,* but *captured*; . . . an occurrence is not *unprece-*

dented but *precedent-shattering,* as if precedents were glass. . . .

''When reporters are taxed with the stereotyped flavor of much newswriting, they sometimes offer as an excuse that most of their work must be done in haste, to meet a deadline. This does not happen to be a good excuse, however, for it would be easier and faster to use the plain language the clichés conceal.''[20]

(See *Journalese.*)

Come/Go

"Secretary of State Cyrus Vance applied more pressure to the white regime in Rhodesia today, warning Premier Ian Smith that the United States will not come to the rescue of the minority government."

This should be "go" rather than "come." They come to us; we go to them.

You choose *come* or *go* from the position of the speaker. And you choose the same way for *bring* and *take, imply* and *infer.* A visitor *brings* something to me; I *take* something to her. The speaker *implies*; listeners *infer.*

20. Roy H. Copperud, *American Usage and Style: The Consensus* (New York: Van Nostrand Reinhold, 1980), 216.

Comparison

"The grimmer fears are being realized in the Navy launch accident in Barcelona, Spain."

Grimmer than what?

The writer created an incomplete comparison. And why wasn't the writer satisfied with *fear* alone? In fact, the fears were that the sailors on the launch had drowned, so the fears were the *grimmest.*

"It's cold in a lot of places, but not as cold as it is in Rice Lake, Wisconsin, where unofficially it's 60—60!—degrees below zero."

Negative comparison calls for "so" rather than the first "as."

A negative comparison calls for making this "not *so* cold as . . ."

But some experts say the rule is old-fashioned. And Theodore M. Bernstein says it's not a rule at all.[21] I hesitate to substitute my judgment for his, so rather than slink away with my tail between my legs, I'll say what a judge might say. "Noted." Or "I'll take that under advisement."

---

21. Theodore M. Bernstein, *Dos, Don't & Maybes of English Usage* (New York: Times Books, 1977), 22.

Continues

"The price of a cup of coffee continues to make news. There are indications that some price relief may be coming."

"Continue" is a weak verb, signaling that the story to follow has been going on for some time and is not new. Further, there's no need to say something makes news. Everything on a newscast is news. Just tell it.

"The war for Rhodesia continues. A communique from Salisbury says a Rhodesian Air Force plane has been shot down in neighboring Mozambique. The crew—two men—presumed killed. Mozambique is a staging area for black nationalist forces, but this is the first time Rhodesia has announced the loss of a plane over that country."

My belated response: Why start with a limp verb? Let's lead with action: "One of Rhodesia's warplanes has been shot down." I hesitate to start with "A *Rhodesian* warplane" because it's inadvisable to begin a story with an adjectival form of a country's name unless listeners are accustomed to hearing the word. A *Canadian* or a *Mexican* warplane would pose no problem, but *Rhodesian* is not an everyday word. Nor are *Kenyan, Zairian* and many others. In fact, Rhodesia is now Zimbabwe.

As for the last two words of the script, "that country": *which* country?

Controversy

"Congress was told today that the way to minimize oil spills by foreign tankers is to limit the number of foreign tankers sailing in U-S waters. We have reports on the foreign tanker controversy from. . . ."

Belated memo: *Controversy* and *controversial* have been so overused that they've lost most of their effect. Writers who want to punch up their copy insert *controversy* in the mistaken belief that it will improve a story. But almost everything Congress ever discusses is controversial. That's why they debate.

Forget *controversy*. Just tell what happened.

Courtesy Titles

"Late today, the President met with his energy adviser, Dr. James Schlesinger, and later the President said the natural gas industry would work with the government and Mr. Schlesinger to seek legal ways to provide a more equitable distribution of natural gas."

Save "Dr." for the second reference, if there's a need for it. But "Dr." and "Mr." don't go together. In any case, we use "Mr." in only a few cases, such as that of the President, someone prominent who has just died, the Rev. Mr. Jackson, et al.

Not only shouldn't the writer shift from "Dr." to "Mr.," but it's even more objectionable when he does so in the same sentence.

More equitable = fair.

Current Events

"We'll have a report on current White House thinking when it comes to our current energy problems."

Apparently, there's no shortage of current.

Better: "We'll have a report on White House thinking about U-S energy problems."

Dependent Clause

"Although personally opposing abortions and Federal payment for them, Joseph Califano said that as Secretary of Health, Education and Welfare, he would carry out abortion programs if the courts approve them."

The problem is that listeners have no idea who the subject of the sentence is going to be until the eleventh word, *Califano*. By then, it's too late. If we were talking about that story outside the newsroom, we'd use the subject's name right away. So why shouldn't we speak as clearly to our listeners as we do to our friends?

When you delay introducing the subject of the story, you frustrate your listeners, especially when you use a pronoun, like *he*, even before you use the name. Starting a story with a dependent (or subordinate) clause, as this one does, is not necessarily wrong. But the best way to write a sentence is the way we converse. We generally start with the subject, go to the verb, then the object. Try not to use a subordinate clause between the subject and the verb. The closer the verb follows the subject, the easier for the listener to follow. In brief: subject-verb-object: S-V-O.

Although and *though* are attractive ways to start a sentence; they give a hint of a twist: "Though Joseph Califano opposes abortions and federal payments for them, he said that if the courts approve them, he, as Secretary of Health, Education and Welfare, would carry out abortion programs."

"With about a million dollars in campaign funds left over from his unsuccessful bid for the Republican Presidential nomination, Ronald Reagan has set up a new political organization for conservatives."

This script is off to a bad start. First, it's not conversational. When was the last time *you* started a conversation with *with*? (Unless it was "Withholding tax is a big pain.") Second, why should a listener have to wait so long to find out the name of the person who's the subject?

A recent CBS News script:

"Now old and ailing and facing a prison term, former Teamsters Union President Roy Williams has been talking to the government about organized labor and organized crime."

That's a nice touch, ''organized labor and organized crime,'' but the lead isn't conversational. We don't start conversations with dependent clauses. Have you ever heard anyone say anything remotely close to this, ''Now hungry, tired and facing a long night, I'm going to get a good meal''?

Four weeks after that script on Roy Williams, the same program ran another lead-in that seemed, well, highly dependent:

"Now old and sick and desperately trying to stay out of jail, former Teamsters Union President Roy Williams has been telling the government about ties between organized labor and organized crime."

(See *Participial Phrase.)*

Differ From

"By habit, he is an early riser, although this morning will be different than any other, simply because of the fact that he's here in Washington and it is the day that he becomes President of the United States."

1. should read "different <u>from</u> any other."
2. "of the fact that" is extraneous.

Whenever you're tempted to say "the fact that," rewrite your sentence. It's wordy. That's a fact.

A local script shows how easily *the fact that* can be replaced:

"The Reagan administration says it doesn't like the fact that the dollar continues to decline on foreign markets."

Better: "The Reagan administration says it doesn't like the dollar's continuing decline on foreign markets."

(See *The Fact That.*)

Dilemma

"The ultimate <u>dilemma</u> of Presidents, as Abraham Lincoln admitted, is how to control events, rather than be controlled by them."

Dilemma = two equally undesirable alternatives. Try "problem," "difficulty," "predicament," etc.

Because the two alternatives are both undesirable, a dilemma is like "damned if you do, damned if you don't."

Do/Does

"The pardon is the most controversial thing that Mr. Carter is likely to do for a while."

Can someone "do" a pardon? Perhaps you meant, "Granting the pardon is the most controversial thing that Mr. Carter is likely to do. . . ."

Someone can *do* the dishes—and, if you're lucky, the windows.

"What Mr. Carter seeks this evening, as he does his first fireside chat over national radio and television, is a sort of public license."

"Delivers," perhaps, but not "does."

Earlier

"Mister Carter held his first meeting with the National Security Council earlier this morning."

As soon as we hear the past tense verb, *held,* we know that the action has been completed; it's over and done with, it's past. Which means we know instantly that it took place earlier, before the newscast. So the word *earlier* is useless.

(See *Later.*)

Echo-Chamber Effect

"[Anchor]: Winter weather in a small Minnesota railroad town hampered firemen early today as they tried to fight a hotel fire. More than 20 persons are feared dead. ________ ________ reports:

[Correspondent]: In the small Minnesota town of Breckenridge. . . ."

I heardja the first time.

"[Correspondent]: Miss Yoshimura couldn't think of much to say, so she let her lawyers do the talking.

"[Attorney]: We all were surprised at the verdict. And right now she doesn't have anything to say."

There's no need to say what the lawyer says. (Is it true that she couldn't think of much to say? Or was it that she chose to remain silent?)

We never know what someone else is thinking—or whether that person is thinking at all.

Exaggeration

"Back in the raucous and exciting '60s, when we had the greening of America and the radicalization of America, it seemed that everything novel, explosive or new had its genesis in or around Berkeley, California. The Berkeley Free Speech Movement made cussing a common and native American art form."

Cursing predates Berkeley by centuries.

Explain

"James Thorpe, the president of Washington Natural Gas Company, explains that the Northwest has adequate supplies, and we, he says, are experiencing one of the mildest winters on record."

Use "explain" for explanations. It is not a synonym for "say."

He says is in the wrong place. Better: "he says we're experiencing . . . ."

Fancy Words

"The president of a Brazilian coffee growers association says his government should initiate a campaign aimed at reducing consumption there of soft drinks and other imported products."

Why use a four-syllable, Latin-root word when a simpler "start" or "begin" will work?

Save *initiate* for stories about fraternities and sororities.

"The excesses of nature are being faced inexpensively and with certainty by people who utilize the forces of nature."

Utilize = use.

"Mr. Carter's nomination of Griffin Bell as attorney general is being challenged by the Americans for Democratic Action, who say Bell does not possess the sensitivity and devotion to constitutional rights required of a man who must rebuild the Justice Department, scarred by Watergate.

Why not "have" instead of "possess"?

Besides, that sentence is too long and complex. Why not streamline the whole story?

"Carter also said criticism that he will yield too much to Congress is erroneous."

"Erroneous" = wrong.

Does the writer fear that using a short word would make people think his vocabulary is poor?

Short words, Churchill said, are best and old words are best of all. Big words have their uses, but not when little words can do the job. Here are some big words broken down into basic English:

abandon	give up
accompany	go with
acquaint	tell
acquire	get, gain
affluent	rich, well off
appears	seems, looks
apprehend	arrest
approximately	about
ascertain	find out, check
assist	help
attempt	try
commence	start, begin
competent	able
component	part
concerning	about
constructive	helpful, useful
consume	eat, use up
contribute	give
customary	usual
demonstrate	show
described as	called
desire	want
determine	learn, find out
discontinue	stop, quit
donate	give
encounter	meet
exceeding the speed limit	speeding
exhibit	show

extinguish	put out
facilitate	ease, help
function (verb)	act, work, serve
illuminated	lighted, lit (past tense)
implement	do, carry out, put into effect
inform	tell
inquire	ask
institute	start, set up
interrogate	question
inundate	flood
locate	find
manufacture	make
merchandise	goods
numerous	many
objective	goal
obtain	get
participate	take part
perceive	see
personnel	staff, workers
possess	have, own
prior to	before
proceed	go, move ahead
provided	if
purchase	buy
pursue	chase
receive	get
relocate	move
remainder	rest
require	need
reside	live
respond	answer
subsequent to	after
sufficient	enough
sustained injuries	was hurt
temblor	earthquake

terminate	end
transport	carry
ultimate	last[22]

The words on the left have Latin roots. The words on the right are almost all of Anglo-Saxon origin. Anglo-Saxon words are generally short, direct and robust. We want to choose the word that fits best, even if it's long, but when it's a tossup between a long word and a short word, it's usually best to go with the short one. Short words pack more punch. Think about the strength of *love, hate, hope, joy, pain, peace, war, home, earth, sky, sun, moon, dark, light, black, white, hot, cold, heart, mind, soul, fire, ice, wind, storm, force, law, truth, life, words.*

''Short words are bright like sparks that glow in the night,'' says the writer Richard Lederer, ''moist like the sea that laps the shore, sharp like the blade of a knife, hot like salt tears that scald the cheek, quick like moths that flit from flame to flame, and terse like the dart and sting of a bee.''[23]

Big people use little words; little people use big words. When we talk outside a studio, we use short words. Why not use them on air?

---

22. A collection of windy words and phrases—and their simple equivalents—can be found in a grammar and usage handbook: *Working with Words: A Concise Guide for Media Editors and Writers* (New York: St. Martin's Press, 1989) by Brian S. Brooks and James L. Pinson.

Another book that can help take the wind out of writing is *Style: Ten Lessons in Clarity & Grace,* 3d ed. (Glenview, Ill.: Scott, Foresman, 1989) by Joseph M. Williams.

23. Richard Lederer, ''The Best Words of All,'' *Writer's Digest,* May 1989, 9.

Farther/Further

"It snowed in northern Florida, and further south the citrus crop . . . ."

For physical distances, use "farther."

Forced To

"Schools in Cottage Grove, Oregon, were forced to close their doors last November after a property tax levy failed for the fourth straight time."

They did close their doors, but were they "forced to"? Wasn't there any measure they could have taken to keep them open? "Forced to" is generally subjective. How many times have you read in a tabloid about a policeman who "was forced to shoot" a man who turned out to be unarmed?

"The United States was forced by its Navy today to offer a formal apology to Japan because of a naval incident in which a U.S. ship practiced shooting missiles in the crowded waters of Tokyo Bay."

Sounds as though a U.S. fleet sailed up the Potomac, trained its guns on the White House and fired off a demand.

And another recent CBS News script:

"Hungary is one of the few places East Germans can visit, and they're flocking to Budapest, to the West German embassy, asking for assistance, hoping for asylum. The embassy has taken in so many refugees that this weekend it was forced to shut its doors, so the East Germans wait outside."

Did Hungarian troops *force* the embassy to shut its doors? Did the West German government order the embassy to close its doors? I suppose the writer meant the embassy was so crowded it couldn't process any more people, so it locked its doors. But we shouldn't have to guess.

Foreign Words

"The Carter family enjoys a big soiree before the swearing-in."

"Party" is plenty good. (I'll bet a lot of truck drivers don't speak French or carry dictionaries in their rigs.)

Even if a newscaster uses a foreign word correctly and pronounces it correctly, how many listeners understand it? The best policy: *Never* use foreign words—unless you're off-duty.

As Murrow once said (but not to me): "You are supposed to describe things in terms that make sense to the truck driver without insulting the intelligence of the professor."

Sevareid put it this way: Never underestimate the intelligence of your listeners but never overestimate their knowledge.

"This is called the People's Inaugural celebration, and the people paid for it—$25 per ticket for invited guests."

Make it "a ticket" instead of "per ticket" and "50 miles an hour" instead of "50 miles per hour," etc. This simpler usage is that of The AP, which avoids foreign words, even such easy ones as "per" and "via." An exception: "percent" is still with us.

In my haste, I overlooked *invited guests,* which is a redundancy. Guests are people who have been invited. If anyone at a party has not been invited, he's probably a crasher or a reporter.

Other foreign words we hear but shouldn't use on air: *déjà vu* (almost always misused), *carte blanche, tête-à-tête, vis-à-vis,* in *lieu* of (better: *instead of or in place of).*

"In the Middle East, a move toward rapprochement between the P.L.O. and Jordan."

Avoid foreign words. "Rapprochement" generally applies to relations between countries. The P.L.O. is not a state. Better: "The P-L-O and Jordan are moving toward reconciliation."

"The Kaufmans are real estate agents, and they say they fell on hard times recently. 'The choice,' says

Mrs. Kaufman, 'was between paying the synagogue and paying the mortgage. We paid the mortgage.' The suit goes to trial the eighth of February. Mazel tov."

Mazel tov? That's Hebrew for "Congratulations!" How many listeners know what it means? And is the anchor addressing the plaintiff or the defendant? Did the anchor say *Mazel tov* in the belief he was saying "Lotsa luck"? And why would he wish either side luck? We don't take sides.

An authority on Yiddish, Leo Rosten, says that although *Mazel tov* literally translates as "good luck," *Mazel tov* is used to say "Congratulations!" or "Thank God!" "The distinction," Rosten says, "is as important as it is subtle. Don't 'mazel tov!' a man going into the hospital; say 'mazel tov!' when he comes out."

Former/Latter (See *Respective.*)

Freight-Train Phrases

"Veterans of Foreign Wars and American Legion spokesmen criticized the executive order."

"Veterans of Foreign Wars" also sounds like "veterans of foreign wars." So I'd transpose the V.F.W. and the Legion. Better yet, I'd go ahead and say, "The American Legion and the Veterans of Foreign Wars criticized the executive order." "Spokesmen" can be ditched.

"In natural-gas-short Ohio, Governor James Rhodes reversed an earlier energy crisis declaration for the city of Dayton ordering closing of schools for 30 days and limiting stores to being open 40 hours a week."

As a suitable adjective for the ear (or eye), "natural-gas-short" falls short.

"Freight-train phrase" is a term used by Ed Bliss for those long strings of adjectives—or nouns used as adjectives—piled in front of nouns or other unwieldy clumps of words.[24] Bliss, who wrote for Murrow, edited for Cronkite and taught many other people, complains they're not conversational and often not comprehensible.

Noteworthy examples of freight-train phrases have been broadcast on CBS News in the past few years:

"This means that, for the first time, the Soviets may have the capability to track and shoot down from above <u>low-flying</u>, <u>ground-radar-avoiding</u> cruise missiles."

By the time the listener finally reaches the noun, "missiles," he has been overcome by aural overkill.

---

24. Edward Bliss Jr. and John M. Patterson, *Writing News for Broadcast,* 2d ed. (New York: Columbia University Press, 1978), 41.

Also from the same source:

"The White House said tonight an American diplomat will board the Achille Lauro to get a hands-on, personal, no-doubt-about-it, official confirmation or denial about whether any hostage was killed."

A *hands-on, personal, no-doubt-about-it, official* confirmation? Clank!

And another freight-train phrase came rumbling along from the same place:

"Yet another costly, red-faces-all-around, space-shuttle-launch delay."

Clunk!

Full

"Four tons of fireworks lit up the skies around the Washington Monument for a full 30 minutes. . . ."

Madison Avenue may fulfill itself by writing about "a full gallon" and "a jumbo gallon." But a gallon is a gallon, and "a full 30 minutes" is still only 30 minutes.

"The full Senate has passed without discussion the resolution creating a special job for Senator Hubert Humphrey."

Both "full" and "special" are superfluous. If a job is created, it is a special job.

A recent CBS script:

"The man who spent six years in prison for rape was finally cleared, a full four years after his alleged victim admitted she fabricated the entire story."

All years are about the same length, so a *full* year is no longer than 365 days.

Gender

"Judge Martin Pulich prodded the eight women and four men that he wanted a verdict sometime Thursday, and that's what he got."

The gender of the jurors is unimportant in this case and in almost all others. The judge prodded them to return a verdict; he did not "prod. . . that. . . ."

Lest I engender confusion, I should say that *gender* is best confined to grammatical classification of nouns and pronouns. The word I should have used in the memo is *sex*. But who'd want to read a memo about sex?

Get/Got/Gotten

"The Brothers Grimm wrote, in fact, very grim stories in which people got eaten by giants . . . ."

"Were" is better than "got."

In fact is unneeded.

A recent CBS News script:

"Outside the Charlotte federal courthouse is a carnival-like atmosphere, but inside the stakes are very high for Bakker, who could get up to 120 years in prison and a five-million-dollar fine if convicted on all counts."

The *if* clause should precede the consequence clause: unless someone is convicted, he can't get anything. Stakes are something risked in a bet, a game or a contest. Bakker's freedom is at stake, but he has no stakes.

Someone can get time in prison but he can't "get" a fine. He could *be* fined and he could *pay* a fine.

It's advisable to pass up *get* in favor of a specific verb. Too often we're willing to settle for *get* instead of searching for the right verb. Finding it may be hard, but that's why writers are so highly paid. (That ought to get you.)

We do say someone is *getting* married or divorced. So if it's acceptable to say someone got married or got divorced, is it also acceptable to say someone got born or got buried? Who ever said English makes sense?

As for "She has got a cold," *has got* is redundant. All we have to say is, "She has a cold."

When grammatical purists hear various uses of *get* and *gotten,* they get upset. But Theodore M. Bernstein tells them to *get lost:* "Trying to get rid of some of these meanings will get you nowhere; they have gotten to be too well established in the language. Get it?"[25]

Good Writing

"The situation in the far south of Lebanon, where rightists and Palestinians have been clashing off and on for months, now stands somewhere <u>between heavy rhetoric and light combat</u>."

Well said!

Writer: Mike Lee.

Why did I choose that script? Its originality. The writer came up with a metaphor that I had never heard before. Writing under the gun, he could have fallen back on a cliché. Instead, he told a much-reported story in a creative way. Sometimes our efforts at originality fall flat, but if we don't try—and fail once in a while—we bore ourselves and our listeners.

Yes, *situation* in the script is hollow. Stronger: *conflict.*

What constitutes good newswriting? Writing that's clear, concise, understandable and graceful. Writing that flows so smoothly and naturally we're not conscious it's

25. Theodore M. Bernstein, *Dos, Don'ts & Maybes of English Usage* (New York: Times Books, 1977), 93.

writing, writing that says something. Our job is not to write writing, even if we could. In journalism, our job is to write reporting.[26] So no matter how well we write, if we don't have facts, we have nothing to write, nothing to report.

"We have called this the year winter ran amok. And there's more proof of it today. It snowed in Dallas, Texas, and the National Weather Service predicts there'll be white stuff on the ground in Louisiana, Mississippi, Alabama and Georgia, and it won't be cotton."

Good. I was getting ready to pounce on "white stuff" as a cliché, but as I went on, I found lead had been transmuted into gold. Well done.

Writer: Morton Dean.

"While half of America is bundling up against the frigid cold wave . . . Australians are sweating through a HEAT WAVE. It's summer 'down under': 105 degrees in Sydney yesterday, down to a comfortable 77 today. Scores of women defied beach regulations . . . taking off half their bikinis to sunbathe TOPLESS.

Around here . . . going topless outside means taking off your HAT."

---

26. Melvin Mencher, "Journalists Should Find 'Truth'/Before Search Starts for Beauty," *Journalism Educator,* Spring 1987, 11.

Good.

Writer: Dan Raviv.

"In El Paso yesterday, it got down to 31, enough to shrivel a jalapeno."

Good line.

Writer: Hughes Rudd.

"It's cold comfort, no doubt, that the United States isn't alone in shivering through an unusually cold winter."

Good.

Writer: Bruce Dunning.

"And when will we see an end to this record-breaking cold? Tomorrow and tomorrow and tomorrow, the forecast is for more of the same."

Good line (with a nod to the Bard).

Writer: David Culhane.

I dragged in the Bard just to make 'em think I'm well-versed.

"Despite all the talk about coffee boycotts, another coffee price hike may be brewing."

Good.

Writer: Mike Whitney.

"France . . . responding to U-S criticism of its release of Palestinian leader Abu Daoud . . . said today, in effect, mind your own business."

Well said.

Writer: Alison Owings.

I wish the subject, *France,* and its verb, *said,* were closer, but I did like the blunt *mind your own business.*

"Banks in Montreal are greeting customers speak-easy fashion today—letting one at a time in through locked doors. The reason is a police slowdown . . . ."

Good.

Writer: Reid Collins.

"There's more handwriting on the walls in China calling for the political rehabilitation of purged

Vice Premier Teng Hsiao-Ping—and suggesting a power struggle among Chinese moderates."

The phrase *handwriting on the walls* is good because at that time some Chinese were scrawling political slogans on walls. But *suggesting* is ambiguous. It can mean the handwriting is hinting at a power struggle, or it can mean the handwriting is proposing a power struggle.

"The Federal Trade Commission charges that the dental profession not only fixes teeth . . . it fixes prices."

Good line (with bite).

Writer: Morton Dean.

"Chances are that very few people noticed it at the time, but every electric clock in the eastern United States ran 28 seconds slow during last week's cold spell, not to be confused with this week's cold spell. Ron Mortenson, project supervisor for the Omaha Public Power District, says it happened because of an overload of electric generating capacity. Mortenson says the slowdown began about six a.m. Eastern Standard Time on Monday, January 17th. So if you were 28 seconds late to work that morning, now you know why."

Good.

Writer: Dallas Townsend.
A complex story told crisply.

" 'Roots'—the book, the dramatization—is popular culture's psychological phenomenon of the decade. The audience ratings testify that the fascination grips American whites as well as blacks. For the latter, explanations are easier, if tentative and partial. At its core, the so-called black revolution in America in this generation has to do primarily with human pride, then with legal rights and economic opportunities as they affect human pride. Pride, when denied, is an explosive force. And events in half the modern world demonstrate that. There was always one element missing in the American blacks' thrust for identity—a sense of continuity. They could not know who they are until they knew who they were. Without that. . . ."

Good line.

Writer: Eric Sevareid.

"Gary Gilmore now has only six more sunrises to see."

Good lead.

Writer: Richard Threlkeld.

"In Henderson, Kentucky, 12-year-old Chris Cleveland underwent surgery yesterday because a ticking sound was coming out of his stomach. Chris, of course, had swallowed a watch 24 hours before he wound up in the hospital. Seems odd that John Cameron Swayze never thought of that for one of his TV commercials."

Good line.

Writer: Hughes Rudd.

You might find his line more timely if you recall the Timex slogan: "Takes a licking but keeps on ticking."

Whenever I read Hughes' scripts, I knew I'd find some well-written copy and some well-turned phrases. I also ran into some longer pieces that struck me as good. Hughes Rudd in particular has an ability to spin a story so that even a long piece seems short.

That's like Milton Berle's tribute to Bishop Fulton J. Sheen, whose half-hour network TV program ran head-to-head with Berle's. Berle said, "When I talk for one minute, it seems like a half hour; when Bishop Sheen talks for a half hour, it seems like one minute."

The following reprinted transcripts are features, sidebars or commentaries, not spot news. Perhaps they stood out because the writers had more time and opportunity to tell their stories in a leisurely, conversational way. Though you and I might quibble about a few points, they are well written and they read as well as they sound. They may run long, but they read short.

Hughes Rudd, "CBS Morning News," Jan. 28, 1977:

"And it's an old tradition in the news business to pick the not *[sic]*—the top news stories every year—that's—which is an exercise of interest only to people in the news business, and one which is, for 1976, mercifully behind us. But a newspaper man named Norm Carter of the Fort Wayne, Indiana, *News-Sentinel* got to worrying about what news stories qualified for the bottom of the list for 1976, and he came up with this one. A woman named Abigail Larp has devoted her entire life to bringing back prohibition. In 1968, in fact, Carter says Ms. Larp went all the way to St. Louis just so she could haul off and slap one of the Budweiser horses. [Laughing] But anyway, last July Fourth, Ms. Larp was on her way to a WCTU picnic when she ran across a man named Burley Parker lying in an alley. Ms. Larp thought that Parker had suffered a heart attack, so she began giving him mouth-to-mouth resuscitation; but actually, Parker had just drunk a fifth of White Port and fourteen bottles of beer, in connection with the Bicentennial celebration, and while Ms. Larp continued her mouth-to-mouth resuscitation, Parker gradually sobered up, but Ms. Larp got drunk. [Laughs] And when she finally arrived at the WCTU's temperance picnic, she somehow got the idea she was in the laundromat, dropped two quarters into the WCTU's secretary's mouth, pulled off her own blouse and washed it in a big bowl of lemonade.

"Well, Norm Carter thinks that qualifies as the rock-bottom story of 1976, and he's probably right. [Laughing] As for those skeptics among you who doubt that the whole thing ever happened, we can only repeat what every grizzled reporter knows: the world is a very strange place, indeed. At this very moment, there is a movement afoot in the Lone Star State to have a canyon near Weatherford incorporated as the town of Buck Naked, Texas. When things like that are going on, anything is possible, even Ms. Larp and Burley Parker, and we'll be back Monday. Thanks."

Rudd again.

Hughes Rudd, "CBS Morning News," Jan. 31, 1977:

"And we have reports here on a couple of scientific experiments in progress, one of which sounds pretty dull, and the other pretty lively, if you're interested in drunk pigs, and, of course, who is not? The dull one is taking place in England, which won't surprise the French and probably won't even surprise some Englishmen. The Ministry of Defence over there is putting volunteers in a dark room for hours and making them watch a television screen on which almost nothing ever happens. John Leonard of the *New York Times* seems to have this sort of experience all the time, as do a number of other television critics, but the British are not interested in what the critics think. They're trying to find out what sort of personality is best suited for watching a radar screen on which almost nothing ever happens. Apparently they don't have soap operas on British television, so the Ministry of Defence shows its volunteers a videotape of an empty landscape, the idea being to find out what sort of people would make good watchers of radar screens aimed at the Soviet Union's missile batteries. If a Soviet missile ever appears as a blip on the British radar, the Ministry of Defence would prefer that the screen-watcher not be asleep at the time, of course, although, if you ask us, that might be the best way to go, but, anyway, that experiment isn't finished yet, so let's get on to the drunk pigs. The pigs involved are drinking alcohol and orange juice at the University of Missouri at Columbia, a school with a certain tradition for this sort of thing, even though members of Sigma Alpha Epsilon are not involved in the present case. The experiment's being run by the U.S. Department of Agriculture for a study of alcoholism among human beings, but they picked pigs as subjects because they say pigs are so much like people in their social behavior. Again, this will be no surprise to John Leonard of the *New York Times* and other observers of the human condition, but the big news about the drunk pigs is that each herd of pigs has a head pig, and when the head pig gets on the sauce, all the other pigs lost *[sic]* their respect for him, even though the other pigs are getting just as drunk as he is. Well, the moral there is pretty clear as far as folks are concerned. When there is an office party, the boss should send his regrets and stay home watching nothing happening on television— and we'll be back tomorrow."

Rudd revisited.

Hughes Rudd, "CBS Morning News," Jan. 27, 1977:

"Well, that's a tough act to follow, but there's a sharp-eyed public relations man here in New York City who is forever on the lookout for oddities in his trade—or anybody else's—named Sanford Teller. And Teller's latest find is a story in the latest issue of *Advertising Age* magazine—a story which is liable to alter a lot of lifestyles on Madison Avenue. The item says that the United States Marine Corps is planning to run a series of ads in advertising magazines, telling the people who put together ads involving the Marine Corps that they don't know a shoepack from an entrenching tool. Apparently, somebody runs an ad every once in a while showing marines doing something or other, such as storming a beach or guarding an embassy, and the Corps says the ads usually get things wrong. So, the Corps has set up a basic training course for advertising people, with Major Arthur Schmidt in charge down in Washington. At the moment, there's no plan to haul the Madison Avenue crowd off to Parris Island to shape them up, which seems a pity in a way, since most of the advertising people we know are desperately in need of haircuts, for one thing. And most of them can't sprint up three steps from a basement French restaurant to street level without blowing like a sperm whale. As far as dress goes, boot camp wouldn't make all that much of a change in their lives; a lot of them are already gotten up in stretch denim fatigue suits with chains around their necks, even though the chains have gold medallions dangling from them instead of dog tags.

"As for training in jungle survival, the advertising boys wouldn't need that at all. If you can survive on Madison Avenue, you can survive anywhere, as long as the martini re-supply choppers can make it into the L.Z. There would, of course, be a problem for the advertising people in getting adjusted to the Corps' way of handling casualties. The Marines take their dead and wounded out with them. On Madison Avenue, they just put them in the bar car of the five-fifteen to Greenwich, and don't even bother to send a note of condolence to the family or to the mortgage holder.

"War and advertising are *both* hell, and we'll be back tomorrow. Thanks."

Rudd redux.

Hughes Rudd, "CBS Morning News," Feb. 1, 1977:

"And, there's trouble and vexation all over the place, no question about it. Take the Amico company of Philadelphia. Amico makes a radio which looks like a cheeseburger, for reasons which absolutely nobody can explain to our satisfaction, and, as though that weren't vexatious enough, it turns out that Windsor Industries of Melville, New York, makes a radio which looks like a hamburger. Well, that was enough to bring on the lawyers right there, of course, and it did. The cheeseburger radio crowd sued the hamburger radio crowd, and the whole thing wound up before a United States District Court judge in Philadelphia. Yesterday, the judge ordered the hamburger radio people to change the name of the hamburger radio to something else, although he didn't say what, and, offhand, we can't think what you could call a radio which looks like a hamburger, if you can't call it a hamburger radio. But that's not the judge's problem, of course; he probably just went home and said to his wife, 'My God, make me a double martini! You can't imagine the kind of day I've had!' But the hamburger radio people have big trouble. About the only suggestion we can make is that they shut down the production line, design new dies and molds and start turning out taco radios or knish radios or maybe hot-dog-with-sauerkraut radios. If there's a market for hamburger radios and cheeseburger radios, by golly, there's a market for absolutely anything. That's an axiom in American politics, of course, as well as in American business, which is just one reason why the country seems to be going to hell in a handbasket. If somebody doesn't come out with a radio shaped like a peanut butter sandwich by the time baseball season starts, we'll be very much surprised. And we'll also be back tomorrow. Thanks."

Bruce Morton, "CBS Morning News," Jan. 20, 1977:

"This is Jimmy Carter's day, of course, his speech, his ceremony; but it seems wrong to start it without saying a little, at least, about Gerald Ford. He never set out to be President. He set out to be the Congressman from Grand Rapids, Michigan; and he hoped to end his career as minority leader of the House. Instead, he became an accidental Vice President, then an accidental President, and probably nobody was more surprised than he. Any assessment of the Ford Presidency has to start by remembering how bad things were when he took over. The Vice President had resigned in disgrace; the President had resigned in disgrace; and the voices of suspicion and rancor and cynicism were very loud. It was, to understate the case, a rotten time. You can argue about the specific things that Gerald Ford did—economic policy, detente, the Nixon pardon—but there's no argument that it is now a better time. And if the man in charge gets the blame, then he ought to get the credit, too. The Nixon White House gave us Charles Colson, who said he would walk over his grandmother to get Richard Nixon re-elected. It gave us a football-fan President who seemed to believe, with Vince Lombardi, that winning was the only thing, or with the Redskins' George Allen—that losing is like dying. Gerald Ford learned his football at a different school. Ford genuinely seemed to believe what football coaches used to teach—that playing the game is important, and that honesty and courtesy matter. The picture we got was of a more relaxed man who could ski and fall down and dance and smile. Offensive linemen—Ford was a center—are team players, some sports psychologist wrote once. Ford was one of those. And unlike some recent Presidents, even seemed to believe that the team could get along without him. He lost the election with dignity and class. Washington film editors see the worst of everybody—the reporter trying 12 times to get his 15-second on-camera close right, the politician bumbling his way through a speech. They have harsh nicknames for most of us, but the nickname they had for Jerry Ford those first few days of his Presidency was different—they called him the 'Grown-up.' "

More Morton.

Bruce Morton, "CBS Morning News," Jan. 31, 1977:

"President Carter said yesterday that he was wearing long underwear and that it was cold in the White House. With the thermometer set at 65 degrees, it was cold in our house, too. The problem wasn't really cold in general—it got up to 30 or so yesterday, colder than usual for Washington, but not unbearable—the problem is that Washingtonians, like other Americans, aren't used to being cold indoors. After all, we practically invented central heating. If we want to know how to survive with the heat shut down, we should go ask the people who never had any in the first place. We should go ask the British, who think being cold indoors is the way life is supposed to be. The Romans had a kind of central heating, circulating heated water through their houses. And Winston Churchill wrote in his *History Of The English Speaking Peoples* that there was more central heating in Britain when it was part of the Roman Empire than at any time through the end of World War II. The British know all about how to be cold indoors; and since they often feel inferiority when dealing with America, they would probably love to send a peace corps over here to show us how it's done. One of the things the British still enjoy—enjoy doing is reading aloud to one another. I remember when I lived there a dozen or so years ago a letter to the editor of *The Daily Mail* asking how to do this comfortably inside one's cold house. Well, the answering letters just poured in, a flowering of British technical invention. Special mittens, somebody suggested; hand-warmers; read aloud in bed under blankets with a special hole so that just the hand holding the book would be exposed to the cold; marry a warm-blooded wife and have her read aloud; and so on and so on. Not one, not a single one, of the 200 or so letters published on this subject ever suggested heating the house. That seemed quaint then, but it really just proves how far ahead of their time those British were."

Bernard Redmont, "The World Tonight," Jan. 12, 1977:

"Soviet author Constantine Potovsky wrote that however long you live in Russia, it never ceases to astonish you by its contrast. First to send a man into space, but Soviet elevators still crawl, creak and break down. Russia is making some precision computers, but almost every shop still uses the abacus instead of a cash register or calculator. It has the world's lowest rents, low income tax, low travel costs. But a good Western-quality suit doesn't exist except for the privileged. And a poorly-made Soviet suit or boots can cost close to a month's pay. A black-and-white TV set sells for four or five hundred dollars, and a subway or bus ticket is about five cents. An average Soviet industrial or office worker, let's call him Ivan Ivanovich, earns 150 rubles —that's about 190 dollars a month at the artificial official rate. Currency experts say the ruble is really worth only one-fifth of that. Ivan pays only five percent of his salary for rent, although his flat is tiny. His medical and dental care are free. Ivan's wife pays about 35 dollars for the simplest dress. Her shoes cost up to 40 dollars. Meat, when available, a dollar to a dollar 50 a pound. Eggs, 15 cents apiece. Potatoes five cents a pound. Bread 20-25 cents a loaf. After years of famine and war's privations, Ivan now gets enough to eat. In fact, he's often overweight from too much bread and potatoes. Fresh fruit, salad and vegetables are short, even in summer. Queuing is a national pastime. Major distribution headaches plague the economy. One day it will be scarce Turkish towels, another day dinnerware. Another day, oranges provoke a buyers' rush. A long-playing Soviet classical record costs about a dollar. But some hard-to-get foreign pop records are selling at 50 dollars on the black market. Bernard Redmont, CBS News, Moscow."

Redmont recently recalled the visit of William L. Shirer to Redmont's journalism class (1939) at Columbia University. Someone asked Shirer, a CBS News correspondent, how long it had taken him to write a 1 1/2-minute spot from Berlin. Shirer's reply: "Twenty years."

Rod MacLeish, "CBS Evening News," Jan. 30, 1977:

"The Tass article—which was, incidentally, Moscow's first snarl at the new American Administration—shows that even the most dismal of autocracies can become sensitized to international criticism. That's an improvement over the years of Hitler and Stalin, who didn't care what anybody thought as they went about savage repression of their own and other countries' citizens.

"Doubtless, protest from around the world saved the life of Alexander Solzhenitsyn, the exiled Soviet novelist. Protest may be keeping Dr. Sakharov out of jail. But, as heaven and numberless victims know, the cause of human rights still needs all the help it can get.

"The ancient degradation of torture is still in common practice. In recent years, protest against it has focused on Chile and Iran. There are insistent claims that genocide is being practiced on Indians in Paraguay. The butchery of Ugandans by their unbalanced dictator, Marshal Idi Amin, is an international scandal. The list goes on and on and revolts civilized sensibilities.

"Human rights are now codified into international law. That's what the Universal Declaration of Human Rights is all about. But such laws are more ideal in their intentions than they are enforceable in daily life. Governments are still considered sovereign within their own borders. Economic or even military threats work only when applied by powerful nations against small, dependent ones.

"So what we are left with is international moral protest against the torture chambers, firing squads, exile and the claustrophobia of fear. Even though we know that such protest cannot be totally effective, we have to go on with it. Society, like our own lives, is always in the process of becoming, and the process itself is the guiding light in a world more familiar with pain than compassion."

Has/Have

"And Congress will have emergency gas legislation sometime this week, which would temporarily lift federal price ceilings on gas transmitted to the East from gas-producing states in the West as a means of making more gas available. Government and industrial analysts, as well as President Carter, are urging gas conservation to ease the industrial gas situation, which has caused at least 200-thousand layoffs so far."

As a verb, *have* is a have-not. It means *own* or *possess.* But used in other senses, it's weak. No drive, no action.

"Congress will *have* emergency gas legislation" is open to at least three interpretations:

1.) Congress will receive the draft of a bill from somewhere or other;

2.) Congress will generate a bill on its own;

3.) Congressional researchers will find long-lost legislation already on the books.

Instead of *have,* the verb the writer should have used is *consider, pass* or *push through.*

Another problem: too much gas.

Hasty Generalizations

"Everybody likes ceremony."

Avoid easy generalizations. I, for one, don't like ceremony, and I know many people who don't. I can just see thousands of people listening to this line and shaking their heads (but not in unison).

"Maybe it's just our own fantasy, says one local long-time resident, but most of us here really think of this as a small town. And to prove it, we all gossip a lot."

The script has no need for "local." When you're writing about a resident of a town, "local" is superfluous.

If "we" was uttered by the resident, the last sentence needs attribution. If "we" here means you and the rest of us, it's overstated because not all of us gossip a lot, whether small town or big city.

Whenever I hear *we,* I wonder who *we* are. Remember the Lone Ranger and Tonto? Surrounded by Indians, the Lone Ranger turned to Tonto: "Looks like we'll have to fight our way out, Tonto." Tonto's retort: "Who's 'we,' white man?"

And a recent CBS News script:

"And while the Air Force was hard at work in the air, they were hard at work on the ground, expressing the latest U.S. point of view with a story guaranteed to win the hearts and minds of everyone."

Everyone? And how can the correspondent say the U.S. story is *guaranteed* to succeed? *Win the hearts and minds*? Haven't we heard that one before?

Homophones

"Henry Ford the Second has resigned from the board of trustees of the Ford Foundation. The auto magnate did so saying the philanthropic organization has spread itself too thin and that its staff often failed to appreciate the capitalist system that provided the money the foundation gives away. . . ."

"Magnate" is not an air word for a couple of reasons. One is that it's a homonym.

I should have pointed out that *auto magnate* sounds like *auto magnet.*

And I should have called them homo*phones,* which are words that sound alike but differ in meaning, spelling and origin. *Homonyms* are words that sound alike and differ in meaning but often have the same spelling.

Careful writers have what you might call homonymophobia. They deal cautiously with homonyms (and homophones) lest they confuse listeners. For example: *Seoul/sole/soul, to/too/two* and *holy/holey/wholly.*

A newscaster recently said *comity,* and I heard *comedy.* The newscaster used it properly, but he shouldn't have used it at all. How many listeners know its meaning? How many newswriters do?

"An Interior Department report on Teton Dam is still pending; so are Congressional studies of the Bureau of Reclamation and other dam-building agencies."

"Dam-building agencies" sounds like a curse. If you read your copy aloud to yourself before turning it in, you'll catch seemingly innocent combinations of words that sound damning.

Hopefully

"Officials here are quoted as saying that the infusion of more Arab forces to the south will hopefully complete efforts for a total ceasefire."

"Hopefully" = with hope. It does not mean "we hope" or "they hope" or even "it is to be hoped." It is widely misused, in fact, almost invariably misused. This is one correct example: "He set out hopefully for Damascus."

Host

"Today Mr. Carter is hosting a meeting in Plains, Georgia, dealing with economic matters."

"Host" is a noun, not a verb.

Other nouns careful writers don't use as verbs: *author (authored), ax (axed), gift (gifted), guest (guested), impact (impacted), mentor (mentored), message (messaged), parent (parented).*

Huh?

"This week's riots seemed a graphic illustration of just how critical the economic crisis in Egypt really is."

A critical crisis?

"Today, at least, evaders were putting up a united front here with deserters, who now face an uncertain future."

We all face an uncertain future.

"They're seeking unconditional amnesty for all veterans who evaded service or deserted to protest the war."

Veterans are those who have served. Someone who evades service is not a vet.

If my copy had been vetted, my first sentence would have been shortened—with the deletion of *are those who.*

"Good land and the underground Ogalala were nature's gift to the High Plains and made them bloom. But the water is running dry.

I've heard of tanks running dry, and wells, supplies, reservoirs, etc. But water running dry? Water does run out, though.

Rivers run dry.

"Dr. Kroger says even the most veteran stars are still troubled."

No one can be "most" veteran.

Veteran is enough.

"He said, cut back on the government rules and regulations that are driving small business people up, and sometimes to, the wall."

Wouldn't one go "to" a wall before going "up" it? I see what you're up to, but somehow I see a film running backward.

Listeners who try to unscramble that picture—and script—wind up talking to themselves and missing what follows. The illogical sequence parallels that of the cliché "He wants to have his cake and eat it, too." Wouldn't it make more sense to say, "He wants to eat his cake and have it, too"?

This from major-market all-news radio:

"Cotton Thomas will always remember the symptoms . . . His ears were burning, he couldn't hear, and it hurt way down deep inside. Not an attack of malaria, but all for the glory of the Roswell, New Mexico, chili-eating contest. Thomas only ate one, but it was a habanero chili pepper, and it went down about as easily as flaming gasoline. And he didn't even win. The guy who did swallowed 17, and it no doubt brought tears to his eyes . . . not necessarily from the victory."

Huh? This script brings tears to an editor's eyes. Not that it's too hot to handle. It's too hard to handle.

Broadcast guidelines tell us not to start a story with the name of an unknown or unfamiliar person, unless we first use a title or a label. So Cotton Thomas needs to be identified. Who on earth is he? A hometown boy?

Always remember? How do we know what anyone else will remember? Let alone *always* remember?

The symptoms the script describes are not those of malaria (chills, sweats, fever). In addition, sick people don't speak of their *symptoms,* and doctors don't ask patients, "What are your symptoms?" Doctors ask, "What's wrong?"

The script calls it a chili-eating contest, then says Thomas ate only one chili pepper and the winner ate 17. So it turns out to be a contest to eat chili *peppers.* (The script says he "only ate one," misplacing the modifier *only.* Should be "ate only one.")

The script says playfully that Cotton's pepper went down "about as easily as flaming gasoline." In fact, flaming gasoline would go down so fast he'd have instant heartburn *and* hotfoot.

The most burning question: Why does the script spend all that time on a loser? Or *any* time on one—unless he's a local? The world doesn't care about losers. Who's the *winner*? If only the editor had kept his cotton-pickin' hands *on*.

"On this, the 10th anniversary of the Supreme Court's re-enactment of the death penalty, state officials say repeated stays by the courts are creating logjams in 38 states that have the death penalty."

This more recent CBS script uses a word, *re-enactment,* that might throw many listeners. The correspondent probably meant *re-instatement.* Only a legislature can enact a law or re-enact one. A *re-enactment* is what police or prosecutors sometimes stage for a suspect who has admitted a crime to make sure he's the culprit. And to pick up more details. But if you hear someone speak of the Supreme Court's "re-enactment" of the death penalty, you might picture the courtly Supremes acting out an execution. Wouldn't that be simulating!

Identification

"Wiliam Proxmire gives a 'Golden Fleece Award' every month for the best example of government waste he can find. January's goes to the Agriculture Department, which spent nearly 46-thousand dollars to find out how long it takes to fry two eggs for breakfast."

Proxmire should be identified.

January's what? January's waste? *January's* should be followed by a noun, *award.* Otherwise, the listener doesn't know what's implied.

If

"Chairman Richard Wiley of the Federal Communications Commission says he will recommend that the commission investigate to determine <u>if</u> the three major networks dominate the television industry."

"If" = supposing that. The word needed here is "whether."

"Officials plan to airlift food to them if there isn't a thaw soon."

In most cases, the "if" clause should precede the consequence clause. Better: "If there is no thaw soon, officials plan to airlift food to them."

Imprecision

"Peking's Kwangming Daily . . . a Chinese minority party newspaper . . . reports today that China has succeeded in manufacturing missiles with nuclear warheads. The Japanese Kyodo News Service reports this is the first confirmation that the Chinese now have nuclear missiles . . . ."

A police state's assertion is not confirmation.

Although the Chinese newspaper was affiliated with a minority party, the government there controls the press.

What should the script have said instead of *confirmation*? Perhaps *public statement* or *semi-official announcement.* What's needed is something more precise. Perhaps a careful reading of the source copy would tell us which word or words would fit.

When we have no specifics, we have to be nonspecific. Rather than make a misstatement, we have to be general. Being concrete takes work, and sometimes we can't nail down specifics. Some writers, though, become facile in blurring and hedging. These practices are derided by a journalism teacher at Iowa State University, Dick Haws:

"Any skillful writer or editor knows that, because of its versatility, 'among' is the utility infielder of hedging. It's the kind of word that can be tossed into virtually any story—and can be defended. For instance, the reporter who's covering the big fire and can't find anyone who knows if this is the worst fire in the city's history can lean on 'among,' as in 'Today's fire was among the worst in the community's history.' All bases are covered with 'among.' The reader comes away thinking a record-setting fire has occurred, and the reporter and editor are happy because they've bumped the story up to the superlative category without ever really knowing if it belonged there."[27] Haws also says "perhaps" is still popular as an easy way to blur the picture.

But our goal is precision. The right word in the right place, hard facts in solid scripts.

"Adamson will attend a final court hearing next week and then begin serving his 20-year jail sentence."

"Prison" is the word needed here; felons go to prison. Jail is where they keep suspects, people awaiting trial and people convicted of misdemeanors. The only person who'd spend 20 years in jail is a jailer.

People convicted of felonies and sentenced to more than a year and a day generally are sent to prisons (which

27. Dick Haws, "Eschew Obfuscation," *Quill*, October 1989, 16.

criminologists, penologists and sociologists prefer to call correctional facilities).

It would be better to say, ''Adamson *is scheduled* to attend a court hearing next week. . . .'' We needn't stick out our necks and say he *will* attend. Maybe he'll kill himself—or be killed. Or get sick. Or die. Or escape.

"The wife of one of Gilmore's victims says she's only worried people will glorify the man who killed her husband."

Widow.

Only?

"The caller promised more bombings unless Britain pulls its troops out of Northern Ireland."

Instead of ''promised,'' make it ''threatened.''

Another careless use of *promise* that we hear on the air: ''The National Weather Service *promises* sunny weather tomorrow.'' The service sometimes *predicts* sunshine, but it makes no promises.

"A decision's due next month on whether Concorde will be granted potentially lucrative landing rights in New York. Environmentalists oppose that idea."

I doubt that environmentalists oppose any ideas; they do oppose landings and landing rights.

"A medical expert intends to decide today whether to resurrect the swine flu vaccination program."

"Revive" is preferable to "resurrect." You revive the dying but resurrect the dead. And "revive" is shorter.

"The Allegheny River today was shut down to commercial barges carrying petroleum and chemicals."

A factory can be shut or shut down, but a river? Try "closed."

Put *today* after the verb.

"It is a closely knit community."

"It's "close-knit."

"In Bremerhaven, West Germany, a freighter loaded with lethal cyanide exploded today, touching off a raging fire, which firemen have not been able to douse. The harbor has been closed and nearby residents evacuated. Police are worried that the cyanide fumes might spread over the city. Three Turkish crewmen are missing and presumed dead in the blast."

"Douse"=immerse or drench; it does not mean "extinguish."

Some dictionaries give a third definition of *douse* as *extinguish*, but we're best off in using the most common meanings of words.

Starting a script with *in* is inadvisable. Once a listener hears "Bremerhaven, West Germany," no one is going to listen up harder, unless he comes from there or is going there.

Better: "A freighter blew up in Bremerhaven, West Germany, today, and police are worried that deadly chemical fumes might spread over the city. The ship was loaded with cyanide, and the explosion set off a fire that firemen have not been able to put out. The harbor has been closed and nearby residents removed. Three Turkish crewmen are missing and presumed dead."

The original script was 57 words. The rewrite is 61 words. Not shorter, but sharper and stronger.

Inflation

"In New Jersey, Governor Brendan Byrne declared war on homeowners who refuse to keep thermostats no higher than 65 during the day and 60 at night."

Please don't declare war on homeowners, crime, crabgrass, etc. Save declarations of war for war.

The script's use of *war* is symptomatic of frequent efforts to pump up a story, especially stories that need nothing extra.

Better: ''New Jersey's governor, Brendan Byrne, is turning the heat on homeowners who refuse to keep their thermostats at 65 or below during the day and, during the night, 60 or below.''

"Reports from Moscow this morning say there was a mysterious explosion Saturday night in a Moscow subway."

''Mysterious'' is a word often put into stories when we don't have enough facts. Or it's used to inflate a limp story.

"The haunting howl of the wolf, mysterious and virtually unheard these days, a howl led by Dr. Erich Klinghammer, a man who's become the leader of the pack."

A wolf's howl may be haunting, but I doubt that it's any more "mysterious" than the sounds made by other animals. "Mysterious" and "mystery" are overused by writers who believe they make a story more interesting.

"Sorensen saw it coming and withdrew his nomination this morning in a secret phone call to Jimmy Carter."

No need for ''secret.'' All phone calls are private unless they're intercepted, amplified or publicized. Calls are secret only if all parties remain close-mouthed and tight-lipped.

"While many prison inmates take college courses from visiting professors, and a few get degrees while behind bars, it is unlikely that any has ever before graduated as valedictorian of his class."

It's a rarity for an inmate to become valedictorian, so I don't think there's any need to jack up the story by suggesting he stands alone. If there were a central registry of inmates who completed college behind bars, I'll bet I could find a few others.

While is best not used as a synonym for *although*. And it shouldn't be used twice in one sentence, especially in two senses.

Ing-lish

"They've been rehearsing other bits and pieces of the inaugural this week: bands practicing playing, troops practicing standing in the cold, and Mr. Carter, we're told, has been rehearsing his speech for the tape recorders."

This plays better without "playing."

The script is also an example of faulty parallelism. Better: "They've been practicing other bits and pieces of the inaugural: bands playing, troops standing in the cold, and Mr. Carter, we're told, rehearsing his speech for tape recorders."

Ing words that are participles—*practicing, playing*—usually are frail. Far sturdier are finite verbs, those with a tense: *practiced, played*. "Finite verbs," according to two keen writers, "are more powerful than strings of participles, gerunds or infinitives."[28] The skill of one of the writers, Robert Penn Warren, was recognized with a Pulitzer Prize—three times.

Initials

"Bell will hear more of that today, from spokesmen for the Congressional Black Caucus, the ADA and others."

For most Americans west of the Hudson, ADA means American Dairy Association. For many others, it's the American Dental Association. Please spell it out for the first mention, then use the initials.

In my memo, *most* Americans should be *many.* And in the next sentence, *many* should become *some.* Talk about learning from your own mistakes!

Except for a few organizations, the full name should be used when first mentioned. Exceptions include A-F-L-C-I-O; C-I-A; F-B-I; G-O-P; I-R-S; K-G-B; N-double-A-C-P; P-T-A and Y-M-C-A.

To make sure the newscaster reads those names letter by letter, each letter should be set off with a hyphen. Otherwise, he might accidentally botch the name.

As for acronyms, words formed from the initial letters of names—*NATO,* for the North Atlantic Treaty

28. Cleanth Brooks and Robert Penn Warren, *Modern Rhetoric,* 4th ed. (New York: Harcourt Brace Jovanovich, 1979), 263. Warren was the nation's first poet laureate.

Organization—it's safe to use them only if they're widely understood.

In Order To

"The Supreme Court said this morning that a community does not have to change its zoning laws in order to make room for low-income housing."

Skip "in order" unless you're paid by the word.

Now that I have time, space and energy, I'll credit that advice to Theodore M. Bernstein.[29]

Interviews

"Mr. Ambassador, if I may have just a word—just one other word. Do you see good prospects for a visit by Mr. Brezhnev this year?"

It's generally best to go ahead and ask your question rather than ask whether you can ask a question.

The ambassador replied, "I think so." That may be diplomatic, but it's not enlightening. When you ask a yes or

29. Theodore M. Bernstein, *Watch Your Language* (Great Neck, N.Y.: Channel Press, 1958), 40.

no question, you give the interviewee an opening to answer with only one word. If the reporter had asked, "What are the prospects for a visit by Mr. Brezhnev this year?" the ambassador would have been required to think and, we hope, say something substantive.

Because of various deficient interviews embedded in scripts, I wrote this item for the weekly *Second Look:*

> Tip to interviewers: Don't apologize to an interviewee for a question you're about to ask, and don't characterize it as difficult. We recently carried an excellent close-up of an important man, but near the end, the reporter said, "Now let me ask you a personal question." This came after several days of many personal questions. But when you tell someone you're going to ask him a personal question, he may tighten up or balk. The best approach in most situations is just to ask your question, but ask only one at a time. When you string several questions together, the interviewee can choose the one he prefers to deal with, then filibuster until you move on to another question (or repeat the question you're especially interested in). Another danger when you ask a string of questions without a pause is that he'll reply only to the one he remembers, or just to the last of the string.

The tip was not published because the committee that reviewed my memos to writers and my items for *Second Look* said that tip went beyond my assignment—to write about writing, not interviewing.

In The News

"The Russian Tu-144 airliner . . . the Soviet S-S-T . . . is back in the news today."

Newscasts consist of news, so there's no need to say someone or something is "back in the news." It wastes time. Just tell the story. It's also wasteful to say that so-and-so is "making news" or "dominating the news." Another expression that's about as useful as a monocle on a karakul is "We begin the news tonight with. . . ." That's like telling someone, "I'm going to say hello. Hello."

Yet another time-waster: "Topping the news tonight." Sounds like Reddi Wip®.

In The Process Of

"While they are in the process of sorting out the nation's economics, Lance and the other Carter appointees are also in the process of rearranging their own financial affairs."

"In the process of" adds nothing but length. Also, ditch "also."

In the process of twice in one sentence!

Jargon

"Senator James Abourezk disagreed with Goldwater, suggesting that would-be draftees who opted out of the Vietnamese War were at least as deserving of a pardon as former President Richard Nixon."

"Opt," "opt for" and "opt out" are bureaucratic jargon. Further, there was no legal option that would-be draftees could exercise. These guys couldn't "opt out" of the war because they never were in it. (See *Vogue Words.*)

"Miss Zigas predicts more than 23-thousand people will be affected by the President's pardon, but she adds a further clarification will have to be made of the President's statement before that number can be finalized."

"Finalize" is a bureaucratic barbarism.

Better: "Miss Zigas predicts the President's pardon will affect more than 23-thousand people. But she said his statement needs to be clarified before the number is firm."

"There was a heavy point-spread against Teng Hsiao-Ping's ever making it back into favor when he was overlooked in the post-Mao power struggle."

Avoid sports jargon.

How many women (and men) know what a "heavy point-spread" is? Further, it's undesirable to use a person's name before identifying him unless he enjoys instant name recognition.

Teng is not on the tip of every tong.

There was a quick snapback to my memo on Teng, which I reprinted in the weekly *Second Look:*

''Avoid sports jargon in a news story? Why? When the argot of the Astroturf can infuse color and imagery into the language, and the parlance of the betting parlor can add a dimension otherwise absent from our dullard dictionary.

''Remember, the item questioned is an endpiece. It is aired on the Friday before Super Bowl XI. A sheltered woman, indeed, innocent of the point spread! Zeitgeist, friend, Zeitgeist.

''As for encumbering the quick, forward lean of the opening sentence with some anchoring deadweight ID such as ''former Deputy Prime Minister of the People's Republic of China''—what a chilling effect that would have on the acceleration of the piece, and what useless information!

''Whether the Chinese put Teng (pronounced ''Dung'') back into government is their business. The suggestion that we throw more of it into our writing is a major concern of one whose style is attacked in the name of pedantry.''

"He will, in the words of someone familiar with plans for the first Carter year, enact moderately liberal programs in a conservative fashion. But even that falls short of the ball park assessment of President Carter gathered by political observers and reporters who followed the Georgian's long trudge toward the White House and the last months in which it turned into sort of a stumbling run."

The Georgian's long trudge is nothing compared with our effort to follow the writer's path.

Sort of a is sorta substandard.

Ball park assessments should be left to assessors.

A more recent CBS News script:

"The morning line on Ronald Reagan: the former President is in stable condition at the Mayo Clinic after. . . ."

An editor should keep a tighter rein on that newscaster. How many listeners know that *the morning line* is a list of entries for a horse race with the probable betting odds? Even if everyone knows, the term is out of place in the script. And many listeners resent hearing racetrack jargon applied, or *mis*applied, to a President laid low.

Sports jargon in non-sports news is almost always inappropriate. Or, as sportscasters would say, *out of bounds.*

Another recent CBS News example of jargon:

"The U.S. and Soviets made their first summit agreement today—to impose a cone of silence over the talks."

How many listeners know what a *cone of silence* is? Even the newscaster didn't know. I didn't, either, but I looked it up. My dictionary's definition: "Space, in the shape of a cone, above a radio beacon, in which there is a sharp reduction in the intensity of transmitted signals." So even if a *cone of silence* could be imposed on the summit talks, it would not impose a total blackout or put a lid on leaks.

Our job is to take jargon and translate it into simple, lively, understandable English. Every trade and profession has its own inside language that can baffle outsiders. So do broadcasters.

A former executive producer of the "CBS Evening

News," Russ Bensley, has compiled a lexicon of broadcasting jargon, so I'm including some samples as a bonus.

Hard news: Well, nobody ever said it would be easy.
Remote pickup: One-night stand in Wichita.
Endpiece: Last remote pickup before airport.
Station break: Transmitter failure.
Takeout: Food to go.
Sound bite: You don't need an orthodontist.
Fast out: Line drive to pitcher.
Bird feed: Sunflower seeds.
Raw stock: Contents of sushi warehouse.
Cold open: Fly unzipped in February.
Nielsen Sweeps: But he doesn't do windows.
Telex: Confide in former spouse.
Character generator: Outward Bound wilderness program.
Prompter copy: What you need if writers are working too slowly.
Howard Stringer: Part-time correspondent based at D.C. university.
Connie Chung and her producer: A lass and A. Lack.
Lane Venardos: Common question from management to Special Events: "Lane, Venardos budget cuts going to be ready?"
Reverse question: ⸮ecyoJ dna retuaS ot deneppah reve tahW

Journalese

"Two cases of swine flu in Wisconsin have <u>triggered</u> a federal panel's call for a limited resumption of the nationwide vaccination program."

"Triggered" is overused. People are triggering too many wars, chain reactions, protests, etc. In this sentence, "prompted" would be better.

Newswriters are also trigger-happy with the verbs *fuel, spark* and *spawn.* Among their favorites: "The increase in the Consumer Price Index was fueled largely by a rise in the cost of housing" and "The storm spawned many tornadoes." When storms are not spawning tornadoes, they're *packing winds* and *dumping rain.*

Let's just pray that no one *sparks* any fuel.

A recent CBS script:

"So Gorbachev's enemies, who hoped the strike would fuel discontent against the Soviet leader, may discover instead that it will give Gorbachev the excuse he needs to boot them out."

I'd change *discover* to *find,* and I'd boot out *boot out* for "get rid of them."

Another favorite of journalese-mongers is *vow.* It's not a synonym for *say.* Newspapers make good use of *vow* because it can be squeezed into a head and takes up less space than *pledge* or *promise.* When a candidate for office says he's going to work for lower taxes or a higher minimum wage, he's hardly *vowing* to do so. When I think of *vow,* I think of a nun taking the veil, an official being sworn in, or a couple being married.

"In general, the tone of *journalese* is the tone of contrived excitement," according to a usage expert, Wilson Follett. He writes:

"When the facts by themselves do not make the

reader's pulse beat faster, the journalist thinks it is his duty to apply the spur and whip of breathless words and phrases. Since these exist only in finite numbers they get repeated, and repetition begets their weakening, their descent into journalese. . . .

"What sense of danger (or, more properly, of a turning point in a dangerous situation), for example, is left in the poor abused word *crisis*? Through frequent and automatic repetition such words find themselves in contexts where they do not belong, hence where their meaning does not come into play except as a signal to routine excitement. . . .

"As for *irony* and *ironic*, the idea of an opposition of meaning between the thing said and the thing intended must be present to make the words applicable. By extension they can be applied to events, and that is why journalese has annexed them. . . .journalese came to use *ironic* for all disappointments and defeats, regardless of their connection with some contrary appearance.

"[Another fault] is the abuse of superlatives—*the most, the first, the only.* These are rarely true, or provable if true; and if true and provable, they generally do not add much to the interest of the subject. If the President's wife receives the gift of a piece of furniture for the White House, it is enough to satisfy any but a childish curiosity that the piece be genuine and of a suitable period; it does not have to be the oldest, most expensive or rarest of its kind. . . .

"In such a mood, it is no wonder that every day some event is said *to make history*. . . .

". . . the misfortune is that in seeking to excite regularly and routinely, journalese does the very opposite of stimulate, and this, it might be said, is ironic."[30]

30. Wilson Follett, *Modern American Usage* (New York: Hill and Wang, 1966), 190.

Kind Of

"And let me start with asking an ignorant question. It's kind of like the oil embargo, in that I think people are of two minds about the shortage, and let me start by asking: Is the problem the fact that the price is controlled, and therefore people hold natural gas back because they don't want to sell it interstate, and so, would removing price controls help a lot. . .?"

All right, already, start.
"Kind of like" is substandard.

"*With* asking" should be "*by* asking."

The fact that should be deleted and the sentence rewritten. (See *The Fact That.*)

Never preface a question by describing it as ignorant. Most of our questions spring from ignorance. Why bad-mouth your own question before you've even asked it? What kind of a signal does that send to the person you're questioning? If it's a dumb question, you shouldn't be asking it.

"It struck me as kind of a sentimental occasion, you know. Even people who normally would never vote with Mr. Ford kind of liked the speech, and it was sort of a cozy evening."

Rubbing out this usage would be the kindest cut of all.

Sort of a, kind of a and *kind of liked* are substandard.

Yes, the same anchor is responsible for both of those examples. I say "responsible" because they seem to have been ad-libbed. They point up once again the hazards of ad-libbing.

Lady/Woman

"School children cheered. Elderly ladies beamed. A horse got spooked."

Ladies are wives of lords. The word needed here is "women." (Remember that line about the maid who answered a help-wanted ad and said to the householder: "Are you the woman who advertised for a lady to scrub floors?")

The last strongholds of *ladies* may be in military officers' clubs, where wives are referred to as ladies. Another holdout: the salutation or reference to "ladies and gentlemen." But even *ladies of the night* have vanished.

Later

"President-elect Carter will meet with the Joint Chiefs of Staff later this morning."

"Later" is unneeded. If someone is going to do something this morning, it has to be later. Use of the future tense obviates the need for "later."

Whatever happens today after I finish this sentence will be later today. It'll also be later this week, later this month and later this year.

Obviate? Why didn't I just say *makes unnecessary*?

Learned

"Recently we learned that Boss Tweed, the supposedly notorious mayor of New York back in the bad old days, really wasn't such a bad chap at all."

The newswriter should have said, "Recently we were told. . . ." Even if the writer had presented it right, he was wrong. So we didn't learn anything.

Tweed was never mayor. He did head Tammany Hall, as the Democratic organization was known, but he never headed City Hall.

Tweed's take as leader of the Tweed Ring in New York City has been estimated at $75 million. He was indicted, convicted (in 1873) and sentenced to 12 years in prison. He died behind bars. *Supposedly* notorious?

The correspondent who wrote that script was a victim of a problem most of us have occasionally: thinking we know something we don't know. Memory is an imperfect instrument, so it's best not to rely on one—yours, mine or a colleague's. Be certain. Check your facts.

Leave/Liberty

[Anchor]: "A tragic end to a weekend liberty leave in Barcelona, Spain, early today. The story from ________ ________.

[Correspondent]: "At least 23 U.S. Navy sailors and marines were killed and 95 injured when a Navy launch rammed a freighter and capsized in Barcelona harbor today. While there was no immediate explanation for the accident, one Spanish port official who witnessed the collision said that the 56-foot liberty launch was going very fast. . . ."

Liberty = authorized absence from ship or station for [generally] less than 72 hours.

Leave = authorized absence [for at least one day, generally for longer periods].

Although the crew was on liberty, except for those on duty and those on (home) leave, the officers were on shore leave, as it's called, rather than liberty. In any case, no one was on "liberty leave."

"Witnessed" = saw.

No need for both the anchor and the correspondent to use *today.*

Lend/Loan

"And the airlines offered to loan 3,000 umbrellas. . . ."

Even if the airlines call themselves Loan Eagles, the verb needed here is "lend." "Loan" is a noun.

And I should have added that "loan" is *only* a noun.

How does this sound to you: "Friends, Romans, countrymen, *loan* me your ears"?

Lie/Lay

"Police say Russell Hart had hidden snowballs in his neighbor's yard and apparently laid in wait for them."

We can't be sure what he might have been doing while he was waiting, but the past tense of "lie" is "lay."

Laid is the past tense of *lay.* The writer should have said the man *lay* in wait or *had been lying* in wait or *had lain* in wait. *Lay* means to put down carefully or to put down flat.

Major

"Mr. Carter said there has been no major breakthrough on efforts to reach an agreement with the Soviet Union to limit nuclear weapons, the so-called SALT talks, but he has been encouraged by messages from Soviet Chairman Brezhnev."

"Major" is unneeded; a breakthrough is major.

Major is a major word in many writers' vocabularies. The best advice: make it a minor one. (Also to be avoided is a *major* milestone. If it's a milestone, it is major.)

But we *can* write about a *diplomatic* breakthrough, a *medical* breakthrough or a *scientific* breakthrough.

An electronic breakthrough of sorts was achieved in this latter-day CBS News script when an anchor asked someone in a live interview:

"Is this seen as a big, major breakthrough?"

May/Might

"The Chicago Tribune reports the late Mayor Richard Daley may have left most of his money in trust funds in the names of his wife and seven children."

The past tense of "may" is "might," so this should read "Daley might have. . . ."

May and *might* have several meanings. For example, *may* is often used to suggest a possibility: "I *may* go for a walk." When the possibility is smaller, it's correct to say: "I *might* go for a walk." It's redundant to say, "I might possibly go for a walk."

For a rundown on *can/may/might,* you may wish to consult a good grammar (but not Grammar Moses).

Middle Names

"Federal Judge Willis Ritter moments ago has stayed the execution of Gary Mark Gilmore. It appears that Gilmore will not face the firing squad at sunrise, but that is not absolutely certain at this point. It's expected that the attorney general of the state of Utah will appeal that stay, and that could conceivably happen this evening. But observers here do not think it will. Observers here do believe that Gary Mark Gilmore will not face a firing squad at sunrise."

Broadcast style calls for the omission of middle names and initials. Exceptions: when there's a possibility of confusion with someone of the same name, and when the person is identified with his middle name or initial, such as John Paul Jones, Booker T. Washington and J. P. Morgan.

In an exceptionally dramatic story such as this, you may be issued a license to use a middle name, but not twice in 20 seconds.

In the first sentence, "has" should be deleted. The rest of the story needs tightening. For example, "the state of Utah" = Utah.

That the live spot was done hurriedly in the middle of the night might help to account for its murkiness [and for six *thats*].

After that transcript and my comment appeared in *Second Look,* another reporter sent me a heated reply. I printed it in the next issue. I kept in the name of our man in Utah because I had asked his permission, and he consented (but I'm omitting it here):

"I come to the defense of ________ ________'s live switch into the 3 a.m. newscast of Jan. 17. Perhaps you are not aware that ________ had just run to a phone, and as I learned later, was not quite ready to begin when he got the cue. CBS News beat all wires on that story by a good 10 minutes. ________ is an excellent reporter. The spot should be viewed in that light and NOT used as an example of poor writing. I'm not even sure it was written. [It was not—M.B.] Your criticism of style, in this case, is grossly unfair."

As the French say, "To know all is to forgive all." But whether that transcript represents writing or adlibbing, it's not good. It underlines the risks in going live and speaking extemporaneously. Besides the flaws I mentioned, the piece had several others. For example: with the word *could,* there's no need for *conceivably.* And the use of *this evening* is puzzling. *Evening* refers to the period between sunset and bedtime, so after midnight, *this evening* would refer to a period 18 hours from then. And who are those anonymous *observers*? Other reporters?

Let's be as specific as we can. Robert Penn Warren, along with Cleanth Brooks, writes: "Use words that are as specific and concrete as possible; that is, never use a word more general and indefinite than is called for. Hazy and indefinite expressions represent the easy way out for writers who are too timid to commit themselves or too lazy to think through what they want to say."[31]

I thought the ad-libber could do better and should have done better. Since then, he *has* done far better.

Misplaced Modifier

"Both the United States and Israel have repeatedly said that negotiations on the future of the West Bank could only be held with Jordan."

Misplaced modifier. This should read, "could be held only with Jordan."

"The agency says the United States is only outspending the Soviet Union in one category."

"Only" should be put just before "one category."

31. Cleanth Brooks and Robert Penn Warren, *Modern Rhetoric*, 4th ed. (New York: Harcourt Brace Jovanovich, 1979), 262.

"An expert on the link between asbestos and possible lung cancer says there are tens of thousands of buildings all over the country that have been sprayed with asbestos."

If the reference is to Dr. Irving Selikoff (or anyone as authoritative as he), the link is between asbestos and lung cancer, not "possible" lung cancer. The link has been well established.

Better: "An expert on the link between asbestos and lung cancer says this country has tens of thousands of buildings that have been sprayed with asbestos."

Moratorium

"But aides claim Mr. Ford has declared a moratorium on any political statements for at least the next 30 days."

We ought to declare a moratorium on "moratorium," especially in reference to political statements.

And it's not too late to also declare a moratorium on *declare*. Too many writers use it indiscriminately as a synonym for *said*. *Declare* means to state officially, formally or with emphasis. Which reminds me of another verb that needs to be used with care: *state*. It means to declare definitely or specifically.

We need to be sensitive to the nuances of words, the shades of meaning that give our language its richness. And we need to read our copy aloud, if only in our heads, to spot gaps and gaffes.

Negation

"No one knows for sure how much of Florida's billion-dollar citrus crop has been destroyed."

It's best to start a story positively. Of course, "no one knows for sure." That applies to much information.

How about this for a lead: "Much of Florida's billion-dollar citrus crop has been destroyed, but no one knows yet how much. One agricultural official estimates. . . ."

Put your sentences in a positive form. Not for nothing do Strunk and White stress that point. Here's a more recent CBS News example:

"The Supreme Court today let stand a California law that says no victim of medical malpractice can receive more than 250-thousand dollars for pain and suffering."

Better: "The U-S Supreme Court has upheld a California law that says a victim of medical malpractice cannot collect more than 250-thousand dollars for pain and suffering."

The nadir of negativity can be plumbed in a sentence with two negatives, as in this local script:

"Police still aren't happy that the man accused of killing a city patrolman won't face the death penalty."

How can a listener sort that out? Even *readers* have to re-read it. The sentence opens on a silly note, that police ''still aren't happy'' about a policeman's murder. How could they be?

Another negative approach, also from a local station:

"No one knows why the dynamite was placed in the church parking lot or who put it there."

Wrong. *Someone* knows. It's just that *we* don't know. The person who did it knows, unless he's forgetful. Even if the anonymous caller isn't the culprit, *she* may know. Stronger: ''Police are still checking the scene for clues to the person who put the dynamite there.''

Another local script:

"There are no reports of damage or injury tonight following a strong earthquake near Los Angeles, possibly along the San Andreas fault."

That opening is common for accidents and disasters. And it's a weak one. Besides the off-putting aspect of a negative approach, *there is* and *there are* are dead phrases. Stronger: ''An earthquake shook Los Angeles (tonight?), but no one is reported hurt. And we have no word of any damage.''

Newspaper Words

"France, its people and its laws, have no need to take lessons from anybody. So said President Giscard d'Estaing today, taking a slap at foreign critics who scored the Paris court release last week of Palestinian extremist Abu Daoud."

Score is a newspaper headline word, a short synonym for *criticize*. But have you ever heard anyone use *score* that way in conversation or on air? In defining *score* as a verb, the *American Heritage Dictionary* of 1969, listing in order of common use, puts that definition in eighth place.

Newspaper words are seldom spoken, except by newscasters. Newspaper editors need a vast store of one-syllable words that can be fitted into one-column heads. That's why we see *hike* used as a synonym for *increase*, and *pact* for *contract*. But I never hear anyone use those one-word synonyms in speech (except newscasters). Would you tell your news director, "I'd like a hike in my next pact"? He'd probably tell you, "Take a hike."

Other words found in newspapers but almost unused outside newsrooms are *youth* and *slay*. Have you ever said, "I saw two youths on the corner last night"? Or "The mob slew him"? Both *kill* and *murder* are spoken, and they're much stronger than *slay*. Otherwise, the Sixth Commandment might be "Thou shalt not *slay*."

Non-Broadcast Words

"The timing of just when fishing may resume remains a question mark, depending upon clarification and implementation of the order."

"Depending upon clarification and implementation" needs rectification.

My commentation needs amplification: I should have told the writer to use plain English, not pretentious polysyllabic profundity.

I should have quoted a master in economy of expression, Hemingway: "The first and most important thing of all, at least for writers today, is to strip language clean, to lay it bare down to the bone."

Papa knows best. But the author William Faulkner disagreed: "He has never been known to use a word that might send the reader to the dictionary."

To which Hemingway shot back: "Poor Faulkner. Does he really think big emotions come from big words? He thinks I don't know the ten-dollar words. I know them all right. But there are older and simpler and better words, and those are the ones I use."

"Among other things, the civil rights group says that while he was an aide to former Georgia governor Ernest Van Diver, Bell recommended and facilitated the enactment of segregationist legislation."

Too many big Latin-root words jammed together. How about "recommended segregationist legislation and eased its enactment"?

My suggested substitute also needs translation into English. Far better: ". . . recommended pro-segregation laws and helped push them through."

"The defense attorney says he will appeal, thus delaying implementation of the sentence."

Instead of "implementation of the sentence," say "the start of the sentence."

Nonsense

"It was a super occasion, but it was not, of course, a super game. It was, in fact, a dull game, proving that football players are human, too."

The game didn't prove anything. As for football players' being human, I think we knew that before the game.

Scrub my "I think."

"Lady Bird Johnson was honored. Norman Rockwell. Maestro Arthur Fiedler. Lowell Thomas. James Michener. Vice President Rockefeller. A Who's Who of achievement that read like the index of an American history textbook."

I wish I had been assigned to read an up-to-the-minute history book that dealt with such interesting people. All I remember from my book was a line on the cover, "In case of fire, throw this in." And a rhyme scrawled in the front: "History is a dry subject, Dry as it can be, First it killed the Romans, Now it's killing me."

I should have been more direct and said simply: Current history books don't include today's celebrities. Some newswriters seem caught up with "history" instead of news. Examples: "Governor Blather made history today," "Washington has taken a historic step" and "History is being written here today." Newswriters would serve listeners better by reporting news. Leave history to historians.

When I reprinted that memo in *Second Look,* I mentioned Arthur Burns, chairman of the Federal Reserve system, in a subhead: "Arthur Fiedled while Burns roamed." Fiedler was the conductor of the Boston Pops; Burns, in his sphere, was a superconductor.

Normalcy

"That his accomplishment was no more a return to normalcy is perhaps the most reassuring development of all, reassuring because it reminds that Richard Nixon was a historical exception, not the rule."

"Normality" is preferred to "normalcy."

Careful writers regard *normalcy* as an abnormality, not an *abnormalcy.*

Reminds is a transitive verb, one that expresses an action that's carried from the subject to an object, so *reminds* requires a direct object to complete the meaning. In the script, *reminds* should be followed by *us* or *me* or *the country.*

Notoriety

"Did you find you had less notoriety outside of basketball than you had when you were in it?"

Notoriety is incorrect. There's nothing shameful about basketball, unless you lose. The word needed is *fame.* Or *acclaim, renown* or *recognition.* Or *respect, regard* or *esteem.* Perhaps *prestige.* Even *celebrity.* No matter which word you choose, even another one, *notoriety* is not the one you need. *Notorious* means "widely and unfavorably known." *Notoriety* is the quality or state of being *notorious.*

Numbers

"Under the Carter proposals, it's estimated that the price of decontrolled natural gas will rise from a dollar-42 to 2 dollars per thousand cubic feet."

It's better when you turn it around and say, "rise to two dollars, from a dollar-42." Otherwise, a listener might think there'll be various prices, ranging from $1.42 to $2.

"Japanese Emperor Hirohito has been given a pay boost. The government in Tokyo is giving him another 80-thousand dollars to run the Imperial household."

"Another" can be used in this context only when the new amount equals the old. Because the Emperor had not been getting 80-thou, you could say "an extra 80-thousand dollars" or "80-thousand dollars more."

Or "an additional 80-thousand dollars."

"When she settles into her fourth grade classroom, Amy will become the first child of a U.S. President in seven decades to attend a public school."

Amy will *be,* not *become.*

Rather than say *seven decades,* make it *70 years.* Many listeners know the meaning of *decade,* but every listener understands *year.*

"Many of Harrison's old 70th Indiana Regiment marched in the parade that year, but there was such a fierce rainstorm that numerous deaths later, in the ranks, were attributed to the outing."

Numerous means *many,* so why not say *many*?

The script seems beyond salvage, but here goes one attempt: ". . . but the rain was so heavy that many deaths among the troops were attributed to the outing."

"Record low temperatures have been tied in recent days in Chicago,and just when it appeared there might be a break in the bitter cold, much of Illinois and the midwest are being hit hard again. Motorists are urged not to drive unless absolutely necessary.

"Much of the area was swept with snow, freezing rain and high winds today, causing low visibility and drifting. Numbers of schools were closed, as well as some smaller airports."

If you can't get the number, just say "a few," "many," "most," "almost all" or whatever fits. Anywhere from 2 schools to 2,000 is a number. (I won't add that if it gets any colder, I'll be even numb-er.) Also, does the writer mean the airports are smaller than the schools?

The first sentence of the script, from a Chicago station, tells us what's already known and probably reported previously, not what's new. Also: much of Illinois and the midwest *is*—not *are*—being hit.

Sentence number two in the script would make a strong opener. At least, it has a note of urgency. If we put that at the top, we should promptly tell *why* motorists are urged not to drive. Perhaps: "They've been warned by police officials that high winds, freezing rain and new snow make driving unsafe."

In sentence three, how could the area be swept *with* high winds? It's the winds that *do* the sweeping.

In his last sentence, the writer should have said, "Many schools were closed, and so were some small airports."

Although I said in my memo that "anywhere from 2 schools to 2,000" is a number, I could have started *before* 2: 1 is a number. So is zero. Numbers have long been a bugaboo in news scripts. The most frequent problems: jamming too many into a sentence or a story and not giving key numbers enough emphasis.

A fairly recent CBS News script:

"After 55 concerts on the road in 20 cities, Michael's glove is going back into the dresser drawer for a while. Since it all began in July in Kansas City, his sequins have sparkled for about two million people. The 10-million-dollar production has taken 1,500 employees across the country with 375 tons of equipment, resulting in a one-million-dollar-a-week budget."

Forget the sequins: the tale is told out of sequence. Pity the poor listeners. How can they remember all those numbers? And why should they? Is $10 million twice the cost of any previous production? Half the cost? If Jackson did have 1,500 employees, listeners might be interested. But *375 tons*? Is that average for a musician's tour? Below average? The tonnage might be worth mentioning if the writer says it's twice as much weight as the Los Angeles Philharmonic ever took on the road. What is a *10-million-dollar production,* one that has a *million-dollar-a-week budget* for 10 weeks? Even if the writer could justify using all those numbers, he didn't present them in a user-friendly way.

Another CBS script:

"An unarmed, four-stage MX missile was launched today from Vandenberg Air Force base in California, and while it was the ninth test firing of an MX, it was the first from an underground silo under so-called 'realistic conditions,' and it took 30 minutes for the missile to reach its target more than 4,000 miles down-range. The Pentagon called the test a success."

What's the significance of *four-stage*? Have all other MX's been three-stage or five-stage? And who cares, other than missile-makers and missile mavens? The *ninth* test firing? Were they all flops? Bull's eyes?

Thirty minutes? Every missile takes a certain length of time to reach a target. Was that longer than usual? Shorter? The distance *is* significant, so why throw off listeners with a batch of chaff, as the military calls strips of metal foil dropped by aircraft to confuse enemy radar by creating false blips.

What's important in that story is that the missile was tested from an underground silo for the first time, traveled 4,000 miles and hit its target. Aside from mishandling the numbers, the writer mishandled all those words and produced a sentence that seems longer—and more complex—than a four-stage missile. As the writing consultant Mackie Morris says: "Avoid numbers. The listener has trouble remembering them."

Another CBS script:

"The controversial MX missile is expected to fly through the Senate today as $1.5 billion <u>are</u> appropriated."

Make it *is*. The rule: A plural noun that shows weight, extent or quantity is—when taken as a single unit—singular and takes a singular verb. Examples: "Thirty pounds is a lot of weight to take off," "Twenty miles is a long distance to walk" and "Ten minutes is not enough time to tour Rhode Island."

As for the missile's flying through the Senate, an editor should have shot it down.

Here's another problem: starting a story about an accident or disaster with numbers. The problem is clear in this recent CBS script:

"14 are now known dead and at least 37 others missing after an apartment building collapsed in southern Italy."

Avoid starting with the body count. Start with the action and set the story in context before giving the box score of dead, injured, missing. Use an action verb, not *are,* which is a linking verb. Linking verbs don't express action, like *hit, shoot, slam.* And it's bad to defer the *where* until the end of the lead.

Stronger: "An apartment building in Italy collapsed today, and 14 people were killed. At least 37 people are missing." Or if the collapse occurred yesterday and was broadcast already, I'd write, "The toll in the collapse of an apartment building in Italy has now reached 14 dead." This version would have the added impact of ending the sentence with a strong one-syllable word, *dead.*

Overkill

"The semi-official Cairo newspaper Al-Ahram reports. . . that the presidents of Egypt, Syria and Sudan will hold a tripartite summit in Khartoum next month."

With three parties meeting, "tripartite" is unneeded. Three parties do not hold bilateral talks. "Summit" is overused; save it for meetings of the heads of the superpowers. Nor should three persons together be called a trio, unless they're acting in concert.

Oxymoron

"This time, however, it's the avant-garde leftists who applaud this $180-million home of modern art, music, industrial design, theater and library, meant to wrest from New York the leadership of the cultural world .... Its interiors, uncluttered by pillars, can handle 10-thousand visitors a day, and are stuffed with millions of dollars' worth of modern old masters. . . ."

How's that again?

An old master is not an elderly painter. An old master is an eminent artist of an earlier period, particularly from the 15th to the 18th centuries. *Modern old master* is an oxymoron, a contradiction in terms, like *old news.*

Overworked Words

My nominees for the 20 most overworked words in broadcast news: *bizarre, controversy, dramatic, exciting, exclusive, first, grim, important, interesting, major, mysterious, poignant, special, spectacular, tonight, tragedy, tragic, unique, unusual* and *very.* And one word that should get no work ever: *meanwhile.*

Use *bizarre* only when it fits as well as it did in this headline in a supermarket tabloid: "I'M MOTHER OF BIG FOOT'S BABY/Girl describes/bizarre ordeal/on camping trip."

A recent CBS News script:

The East Germans lucky enough to make it across know they won't be prosecuted; and more importantly, they won't be sent back."

The use of the adverb *importantly*—instead of the adjective *important* or the phrase *more important*—sounds pretentious, an attempt to make it seem *all-important.*

Participial Phrase

"Smiling in each others' arms, looking at the glittering ceiling, President and Mrs. Carter waltzed to Moon River, played by Peter Duchin's orchestra.

This was written for radio, so there was no footage at the top that showed the Carters dancing. When listeners hear *smiling,* they have no idea who's smiling or what the story is all about. And when they hear *looking,* they still have no idea who the subject is, who's smiling, who's dancing, who's so moony. Why not tell them at the top? Why start a story with a participial phrase and keep listeners in the dark? We're not playing guessing games. The best pattern for a sentence is subject, verb, object: S-V-O.

This recent CBS News script led a newscast:

"Having beamed back a wealth of photos and sensor data on planet Neptune and its eight moons, Correspondent ________ ________ tells us Voyager 2 is soaring into uncharted territory."

If I'd known the correspondent was going off forever, I might have phoned to say goodby. That dangling participial phrase—"Having beamed back a wealth of photos . . . ."—is misleading.

A participial phrase acts as an adjective, so the phrase that starts the sentence modifies the subject—the correspondent. But the anchor intended the phrase to modify Voyager 2. His misstep makes it a dangler.

Undangling the sentence is easy: "The spacecraft Voyager-Two is streaking into uncharted territory, and scientists are now studying the photos of the planet Neptune and other data the craft beamed back. Correspondent ________ ________ reports from Pasadena, California."

A script on ABC News was also astounding:

"As many of you already know, this week the United States is marking a major achievement in space exploration, the fly-by of the planet Neptune and its moons by spacecraft Voyager-2, launched 12 years ago. [Voice-over] This is its last stop in our solar system before heading out into the Milky Way. . . ."

Last *stop*? The spacecraft is going to the end of the line non-stop. The writer and anchor must have known that, but someone—in fact, more than one someone—didn't stop to think.

Another far-out dangler, this one cooked up for a

grammar: "Covered with onions, relish, and ketchup, I ate a hot dog at the ballpark."[32] The sentence can be fixed by making it plain that the toppings cover the hot dog, not the speaker: "At the ballpark, I ate a hot dog covered with onions, relish and ketchup."

How does a grammatical error like that first dangler ever get on air? And how did this mistake get on a recent CBS News broadcast?

"The East Germans, who like to punish families by breaking them apart, allowed Jochan Eicler's parents to emigrate but ordered he and his sister to stay behind."

He? The object of a verb is in the objective case, so *he* should be *him*.

Another type of error on a recent ABC News program:

"The thought may fascinate or horrify you, but what if some day a thousand light-years from now, some alien intelligence decoded the signal."

Light-year is a measure of distance, not time.

Editors are supposed to read scripts for style, grammar and accuracy. But someone, or several someones, dropped the ball. (Adlai Stevenson said, "An editor is one who separates the wheat from the chaff and prints the chaff.")

(See *Dependent Clause*.)

---

32. Bernice Randall, *Webster's New World Guide to Current American Usage* (New York: Simon & Schuster, 1988), 71.

Passive Voice

"The first cabinet meeting gave clues to the Carter presidential style. Snippets of what had been campaign rhetoric came across as directives in this meeting, from the President to his subordinates. Door-to-door limousine service for senior White House staffers had been eliminated. And to the cabinet members, Mr. Carter said, look at your own departments for similar reductions. Look at commissions and advisory boards: There are too many of them. There are too many lawyers making too many regulations. Citing the government paperwork that was necessary in his peanut warehouse business in Plains, and what was described as the oceans of paperwork from H-E-W at his local Sumter County School Board, Mr. Carter is reported to have said, some of these regulations must be there only because the legal staffs are so large and have nothing else to do . . . ."

Eliminated by whom? Use of the passive often raises the question of who did the doing. In this case, it seems Carter stopped the service. But with that construction, it's not clear who the agent (doer) was. In fact, with "had been," the sense seems to be that the elimination of service had been made before the meeting. It would be clearer to say: "Mr. Carter told them he had stopped door-to-door limousine service for senior White House staff members. And he told the cabinet . . . ."

I didn't hear the delivery, but the sentence about too many lawyers might sound as though the correspondent is passing judgment. I think it's safer to put a source at the beginning of that sentence, perhaps "Mr. Carter said."

The first sentence of the script is adequate, but much of the rest needs reworking. One example: *Cite* is a good word for broadcasters to drop out of sight. It's a homophone, along with *sight* and *site.* Listeners don't read your script, and they can't be sure which word you're using until they reach the end of the opening dependent clause. Even then, they might not be able to tell. And they aren't going to take time to puzzle it out.

In my original memo, I used the word "staffers." But in this revision, I've changed it to "staff members." Consultants on a usage panel were asked whether "staffer" irritated them, and 77 percent said yes.[33] I tend to think the majority is always wrong. But now I'm inclined to agree with the members of the panel. One of those irritated, the writer Heywood Hale Broun, said of *staffer*: "It is one with 'newshawk' or 'gal Friday.'" A former editor and book critic, Stanton Peckham, dismissed *staffer* as "bad Press Club jargon." The novelist Herman Wouk said he might use *staffer* in writing "to characterize the speech of a bureaucratic dolt."

Pathetic Fallacy

"The <u>killer</u> <u>freeze</u> ruined the Florida tomato crop."

Weather can kill, but do not assign human characteristics to it. There is no such thing as a "killer freeze" or a "killer storm."

That's an example of "pathetic fallacy," a phrase coined by a British critic, John Ruskin. He used it to describe the attribution of human traits to animals and inanimate objects.

---

33. William and Mary Morris, *Harper Dictionary of Contemporary Usage*, 2d ed. (New York: Harper & Row, 1985), 561.

"This is the worst situation facing migrant farm workers here since 1972, when a killer frost, followed by a drought, killed the crop."

"Killer frost" sounds like a brutal wrestler.

Frost does kill, but frost has no mind, no will. Frost can't go around looking for victims, skulking through orchards, lurking behind hedges, pouncing on the unwary. There can't be a "killer frost" any more than there can be a "killer car," a "killer quake," a "killer disease" or a "killer elevator."

"But the unseasonable cold has swung its fury to the south, damaging Florida's citrus and vegetable crops."

Same problem. This sounds as though the cold decided to shift its attention to the south.

If storms could think, they could also go mad. Then, imagine their fury.

People/Person

"Indications are that somewhere close to one million persons were put out of work by the weather last week, and that the figure may approach a million and a half this week if the weather stays extremely cold."

For large, inexact numbers make it "people."

The correspondent's report needs rewriting because he doesn't stress the key facts: the number of people out of work and the number that may wind up out of work.

Better: "Indications are that the cold wave last week put almost a million people out of work. And if the severe cold persists this week, the number of people frozen out may reach a million and a half."

"As the 26 cars moved through the country, it's estimated that they were seen by 30-million persons."

"People" is the word desired here, not "persons." Use "persons" for small, exact numbers. Use "people" for large, inexact numbers, except when stressing individuality. When talking about the prisoners on death rows, I'd say 355 (?) "persons" because I'd want to stress the individual units.

But I don't use *individuals* when talking about people. *Individual* is a pompous word for *person.*

Most newscasters are *people* persons: They prefer *people* for any number, from two to two billion.

Possessive

"The presence of American troops and those of our allies, he added, are [should be *is*] living proof of our pledge to honor that commitment."

"Our pledge" sounds as though CBS has troops and makes such pledges. That's why it's best to avoid the first person plural, *we,* and the possessive *our.* Even the Voice of America, which is a government organ, does not say "our pledge."

"This is the day Claudine Longet learns the sentence for killing Spider Sabich, the champion skier."

Substitute "her" for "the."

The possessive *her* would have personalized the noun and tied the sentencing back to her.

Prepositions

"Later on, these people will hold a prayer vigil outside the prison."

Off "on."

Prepositions—including *at, by, for, in, into, of, on, to* and *with*—cause many problems, particularly when combined with verbs. Some verbs need their prepositional tails—*look in on, look up to*—but in several scripts we see that the prepositions are useless.

"Egyptian President Anwar Sadat today ordered no mercy for anyone who tries to start up more food riots in Egypt."

Off "up."

Mercy me, that script needs help. A "food riot" reminds us of *Animal House*. The key words, *no mercy*, are set down in the middle, so they're underplayed. And there's no need to tack on *in Egypt*. Where else would the Egyptian president have any authority?

Better: "Egypt's president, Anwar Sadat, said today anyone else who tries to start riots over food will be shown no mercy."

"Congress is rushing to finish up work on the Carter emergency energy legislation."

Off "up."

"The public address system and microphones over which Mr. Carter will deliver his Inaugural Address have been appropriately tested out."

"Out" should be offed.

Appropriately tested? Would the mikes have been tested inappropriately?

"Two elderly men in New York City died inside their hotel residence Tuesday . . . ."

"In" is inside enough.

"He works at the prison laundry, fitting inmates who are being released with civilian clothes."

He works "in" the laundry.

The inmates are probably released *wearing*—not *with*—civilian clothes.

"Reports out of Peking today indicate that Chinese troops have put an end to what is called 'great chaos' in the city of Paoting."

"From" is better.

"At about ten-thirty, the Carters will cross Pennsylvania Avenue for coffee with the Fords, the Rockefellers and the Mondales."

No need for "at."

At about is redundant when referring to time, although it's acceptable for quoting rates and prices.

"During all of the years that Hughes spent in this room, the windows were covered over."

"Over" is unneeded.

So is *of.*

"Two gunmen shot down a prominent Cuban exile leader in Miami today. Juan Peruyero, about 50, was listed in critical condition. Peruyero was a former president of the Bay of Pigs Veterans' Association. The gunmen, firing from a car, apparently got away."

"Down" can be dispensed with. That's one down, one to go. Why "apparently"? They aren't in custody, are they?

After a closer look at the script, I see another problem. "*Was* a former president" should be "*is.*"

Better: "A prominent Cuban exile in Miami has been shot. 50-year-old Juan Peruyero is in critical condition. He's a former head of the Bay of Pigs Veterans Association. Two gunmen got away in a car."

Present Perfect Tense

"It snowed this morning in Miami for the first time since the weather bureau has started keeping records. The same thing happened in West Palm Beach and Boca Raton."

A tense situation; dump "has."

The mixed tenses don't mesh; they grind. The present perfect progressive (*has started keeping*) shows that an event begun in the past continues into the present. The present perfect (*has started*) is handy for broadcast newswriters. It lets us report an action without using *today* or *yesterday.* But this script combines two tenses, the simple past (*snowed*) and the present perfect progressive, plus *this morning.* If you start with a verb in the past tense, you don't shift to the present perfect. And you don't use both tenses in the same sentence.

In the script's second sentence, what does "the same thing" refer to: snowing, record-keeping or snowing *and* record-keeping?

Presently

"The President said he was rejecting the board's decision because some foreign governments are presently dissatisfied with bilateral agreements governing international air travel."

"Presently" = soon. If you mean "at present," use "now" or "currently." But in this sentence, there's no need for any of them.

I should have said *that sentence.*

Prior To

"His supporters, silent prior to the hearing, said he had been treated unfairly."

"Prior to" = before; "subsequent to" = after.

Perhaps the writer meant *until.*

Proposal/Proposition

"President Ford sent Congress a proposition today: consolidate several agencies with similar functions into a cabinet-level Department of Energy."

Proper usage calls for "proposal" here rather than "proposition."

Proposition has its place in certain contexts, but the President certainly wasn't propositioning the Congress.

Quote/End Quote/ Unquote

"I thought that was an interesting quote."

"Quote" is a verb; the word needed here is "quotation."

"In response to a Civil Liberties suit, Federal Judge Willis Ritter frustrated Gilmore's death wish once more, the third time in two months, saying Utah's capital punishment law has never been tested before for its constitutionality. He said, quote, 'There are serious doubts about the validity of the statute.' "

"Quote" is a word to quash.

There's no need to call a cluster of words a quotation unless the speaker said something so startling or unusual that you want to make sure that no listener thinks you're commenting or interpreting. But in this case, you could easily say the words enclosed in quotation marks without announcing that it's a word-for-word quotation. With or without your announcement, the sentence means the same: "He said there are serious doubts about the validity of the statute." The only difference is that the script has that eyesore, or earsore, *quote.* So put a quietus on *quote.*

A more recent example from CBS News:

"Says Dole, and I quote, 'There is just no excuse. Those sales knocked into a cocked hat the credibility of the formal U.S. policy of no concessions to terrorists.' Unquote."

Better: "Dole says there's no excuse. And he says the sales ruined the credibility of the U-S policy of no concessions to terrorists." Putting *says* before *Dole* isn't conversational, and it's not good broadcast newswriting.

Another recent CBS script:

"No details on the charges, but the announcement indicated it involves a, quote, 'compromise of U.S. security.' "

If the anchor hadn't used the word *quote,* the sentence would have read the same, but better. Also, there's nothing distinctive about the words "compromise of U.S. security."

Another CBS script:

"President Bush insisted his legislation, quote, 'has teeth.' "

If you extract *quote* and the quotation marks, the quotation itself has the same flavor.

Good writers avoid *quote, end quote* and *unquote.* And you can quote me. Better yet, you can quote a broadcast pioneer: "Thoughtless use of such hackneyed terms as 'quote' and 'end quote' tend to interrupt the listener's thought. They have a barking, staccato sound no matter how softly they are spoken. They call attention to themselves and detract from the story."[34]

The first news director of CBS News said, "Remember that since the word 'quote' is foreign to the ear as far as ordinary conversation is concerned, it probably always is disturbing to the listener. . . ." And he added, "Please, please don't use 'unquote.' "[35]

34. Burton L. Hotaling, *A Manual of Radio News* (Milwaukee: The Milwaukee Journal, 1947), 25.

35. Paul W. White, *News on the Air* (New York: Harcourt, Brace, 1947), 68.

The quotations we hear quoted on air are often wordy and not worth quoting verbatim. Most should be condensed and paraphrased by the newscaster. If it's essential to preserve the speaker's exact words, which it seldom is, the newscaster can make clear he's quoting the speaker through skillful delivery. Or he can use an attributing phrase. Among them: "In the words of," "to use her words," "what they called" and "as he put it."

Reason Why

"Senility has been given as the reason why a California group wants to remove a state supreme court justice from the bench."

"Why" is superfluous; "reason" is reason enough.

For various reasons, usage experts vary about *reason why*. But most reject it. "There is no question," say William and Mary Morris, "that *the reason why* is a redundant expression and that the *why* is unnecessary. There is also no question that it is an established idiom in the American language."[36]

Bergen Evans approves *reason why* and says, "As a rule, it is better to be natural than to be correct according to theories that other people have never heard of."[37]

36. William and Mary Morris, *Harper Dictionary of Contemporary Usage*, 2d ed. (New York: Harper & Row, 1985), 510.

37. Bergen Evans and Cornelia Evans, *A Dictionary of Contemporary Usage* (New York: Random House, 1957), 557.

Theodore M. Bernstein says: ''When *reason* stands at the head of a sentence, no *why* is necessary . . . .When anything intervenes between *reason* and the clause, a *why* is necessary: 'I see no reason, sound or unsound, why he is tired' . . . .When a negative precedes *reason,* a *why* is necessary . . . .'' And he adds, ''Examination of a goodly number of samples suggests that the *why* is necessary more often than it is dispensable and it is never unidiomatic, and never wrong.''[38]

I go along with the reasoning of Claire Kehrwald Cook: ''Instead of writing *That is the reason why the program failed,* you can say either *That is the reason the program failed* or *That is why the program failed.*''[39] Seems reasonable.

Redundancy

"The reaction in Plains, Georgia, is not that strong but there seems little doubt the Sorensen case is an unpleasant embarrassment for Jimmy Carter in this inauguration week."

''Unpleasant'' is unneeded before ''embarrassment.''

Have you ever been embarrassed *pleasantly*?

38. Theodore M. Bernstein, *Miss Thistlebottom's Hobgoblins* (New York: Farrar Straus Giroux, 1971), 181.

39. Claire Kehrwald Cook, *Line by Line: How to Edit Your Own Writing* (Boston: Houghton Mifflin Co., 1985), 193.

Seems weakens what follows. Don't retreat behind *seems* when you can safely go forward with *is.*

"When advocates of troop reduction learn the true facts. . . ."

"True facts" is redundant. If something is not true, it's not a fact.

In looking back, I should have said it positively, "If something is true, it is a fact."

"Although she was traveling only five blocks in a chauffeured limousine with the First Lady of the land, Amy Carter was late to school, delayed by heavy traffic."

"Chauffeured limousine" is redundant. A limousine is a vehicle built especially for a hired driver; there's usually a partition between front and back. A small car may have a hired driver, but that doesn't make a Pinto a limo.

Does an owner ever drive a limo? Only when the chauffeur runs off with his wife.

The state of Minnesota clearly dominates this crowd, which has filled the ballroom at the Shoreham Hotel to capacity."

"Fill" = put into as much as can be held. So "fill to capacity" is redundant.

Minnesota has been a state since 1858, so there's no need to identify it as a state.

"In Ohio, officials of natural gas companies welcome any temporary deregulation in the price of gas, but they say frankly, it will do nothing to relieve the current gas crisis. Gas officials say the reason there's a gas shortage is because the price has been kept artificially low for years by price controls."

"The reason. . . because" is redundant. Make it, "Gas officials say there's a shortage because the price. . . ."

There's no need to say "gas shortage" because you've already mentioned gas four times in four lines.

"The Japanese, however, had been expecting such an announcement, and it was no great surprise, in line with Mondale's promise that there would be no unexpected foreign policy surprises such as those Japan suffered several times during the Nixon administration. The meetings here were cordial and warm, and Mondale left for Washington characterizing the entire seven-nation trip a greater success than expected in showing that President Carter places priorities on the countries Mondale calls our traditional allies and friends."

Surprise = unexpected occurrence, so you shouldn't talk about an "unexpected surprise."

"Cordial" = warm, so don't say "cordial and warm."

Besides the redundancy (*unexpected surprise*), the first sentence of the script has *two* non-surprises. They've led, unsurprisingly, to another problem: bloat.

"At the National Weather Service and other meteorological centers, learned scientists scan their data to determine how much longer winter will plague us."

"Learned scientists" is redundant. A scientist is someone with expert knowledge [of at least one science].

"In upstate New York, 18 inches of new snow fell on Watertown today."

Inasmuch as snow cannot be recycled, the only kind that can fall is "new."

"Benin Radio says the 'mercenaries' are now 'in flight' from the capital city."

The capital is a city.

"We'll have more on that same story a bit later in the broadcast."

That same is redundant. ''That story'' means the same.

Several recent CBS News scripts:

"The FBI says that he's been given safe haven in Cuba, along with a part of the stolen loot."

Loot is stolen property.

"The three armed gunmen who have been holding court officials as hostages left the building and are at a nearby airport."

Have you ever heard of an *un*armed gunman?

"That's a new record for December and just a half-inch short of the record for any month."

New record is an old redundancy. If someone breaks a record, then that's the record. What my be a record for redundancies in one sentence was set in this CBS script:

"Ten-thousand invited guests are gathering in a national park for the formal funeral ceremonies, and they include representatives of 163 countries, 55 heads of state, but first and foremost among them is the President of the United States, making his first overseas trip since he took office to be present at the Dawn of a New Era."

There's no such thing as an *un*invited guest; a funeral *is* a service or a ceremony; *first and foremost* is fustian.

As a redundancy hunter might say, "Redundancies need *careful* scrutiny because they are *totally* unnecessary."

Repetition

"In Basel, Switzerland, eight leading banking nations, including the United States, have agreed to bolster the beleaguered pound. They will extend to the Bank of England a 3-billion-dollar line of credit—the credit to be used to bolster the pound when large foreign holders of sterling sell the pounds they hold."

I wouldn't use the second "bolster" so close to the first. How about "strengthen," "prop up," "support," or "shore up"?

Bolster is a noticeable word. It stands out. Some words can be repeated in a script without being noticed. For example, *says* and *said.*

It's usually better to stick with a simple word than shift to a synonym that might strike listeners as something else with a different meaning. When writing about an international agreement, for example, don't try to get around repeating *agreement* by writing *accord. Accord* is not a conversational word, except perhaps at the State Department, and many listeners don't know what it means.

This local script shows how some writers will take the long way around to avoid repeating a word that should be repeated:

"Argentine soldiers, backed by tanks and artillery, have regained control of most of an infantry base that alleged leftist guerrillas attacked and held briefly near Buenos Aires. A news agency says at least some of the insurgents were killed or wounded . . ."

Even listeners who know the word *insurgents* may be unsure whether they're the same people as the guerrillas or whether they're another bunch and, if so, how they fit into the picture. So it would be better for the writer to repeat *guerrillas* or use the simpler *rebels.*

Here's another attempt to avoid repeating a word, this from a local station:

"Atlanta Mayor Andrew Young showed little interest today in running for lieutenant governor instead of the state's top office."

The writer would have performed a public service by deleting *the state's top office* and substituting *governor.*

"Franklin Roosevelt was the master. He gave the first Presidential fireside chat back in 1933. The talks were described then as warm and stirring. He addressed the nation as "My friends." Those were Depression days: banks were closed, the nation was on the verge of economic panic. People wondered what the federal government would do, and they queued up in bread lines for something to eat. The President's voice—which went into millions of homes by radio, not television—was warm and reassuring. . . ."

He must have been sitting too close to the fire to get that warm.

F.D.R. might have exuded warmth, but once you say the talks were warm, there's no need for re-warming.

[Anchor]: "United Nations Ambassador Andrew Young is flying tonight to London, the first stop on a 10-day trip that will take him to Africa with major black leaders. Young called it a 'get-acquainted' visit . . . ."

[Correspondent]: "It was arranged as a get-acquainted session. . . ."

The editor, anchor and producer should get acquainted with the copy so the same much-used expression isn't used in two consecutive stories.

Respected

"A respected meteorologist—Hurd Willett—is suggesting spring may be a little chilly this year. Willett is professor emeritus at the Massachusetts Institute of Technology. . . ."

It's best not to call people "respected" merely to validate their expertise. *Respected* is assumed. If he's not respected, you wouldn't be quoting him. Once you start calling people *respected,* you may leave the implication that other people you mention are not respected.

Also: don't describe prizes or positions as coveted or prestigious. Or people as famed or famous. If you call someone famous and a listener has never heard of her, you risk making the listener feel ignorant or inadequate. If everyone knows that the subject of your story is famous, there's no need to call her famous.

Respective

"There's more evidence today of the continuing split between Egypt and the Soviet Union: the two countries using their respective newspapers to attack each other."

"Respective" is extraneous. I wouldn't expect Egypt to use Russian papers or wice wersa.

Respective and *respectively* are words we don't use in a newscast. They require a listener to mentally rewind and match words that have already flown past. And for the same reason, we don't use *former* and *latter* in referring to subjects previously mentioned. Listeners don't keep track of the cast of characters in a story and the order of their appearance.

Rewriting

"The Center for Disease Control in Atlanta said this afternoon that a rare, bacteria-like material which medical science knows very little about is believed to have caused the Legionnaire's Disease that killed 29 people who were exposed to it in Philadelphia late last summer. Dr. David Sensor, director of the C-D-C, said the bacteria, which he did not identify, apparently was responsible for a pneumonia-like outbreak at St. Elizabeth's hospital in Washington in 1966. That outbreak took 20 lives. He said, 'We don't know how it was transmitted but we now know what to look for.' The studies continue."

I think the last line is superfluous. It would be newsworthy if you could write, "But they are abandoning the investigation."

I commented on only the last sentence, but the first sentence also needs work. So does the second. They all do.

The broadcast script discloses the cause of the disease early in the second line, then rambles on for about 30 more words. That's an effective way to *de*-emphasize the cause. The cause is the news, so the sentence should build up to it.

Stronger: "Medical researchers say the Legionnaire's Disease that struck 29 people in Philadelphia and killed them was apparently caused by a rare, bacteria-like material. The researchers—at the U-S Center for Disease Control in Atlanta—also say. . . ."

The Center became Centers in 1980.

I said "struck . . . and killed" because I suspect that not all of them died in Philadelphia.

The original script needs intensive care.

"An attorney in the Howard Hughes will hassle says today that the Utah gas station operator whose fingerprints appeared on the envelope of one purported will in which Melvin Dummar is named a major heir admits now he delivered the will to the Mormon Church headquarters, where it was discovered."

I doubt that even Dummar will get a sentence that long.

Whew! Or should I say *Whews*? Not only is that sentence overlong; it's convoluted. The writer didn't know what he wanted to say; he just plunged in and flailed.

His problem might have been his failure to first think through what he wanted to say and how to say it. But to write clearly, you must think clearly. If the writer of the script had had a clear concept, he wouldn't have written a sentence of 50 words.

A recent CBS News sentence runs even longer:

"In most rural areas of the country, rain's a welcome event, but that has not been the case this summer in the deserts of New Mexico, where more rain than usual has posed a new threat to what could be a disappearing national treasure—the Spanish missions that have become so much a part of the Southwestern landscape."

That's 58 words but far from a record. The longest sentence I've ever heard about—haven't had time to read it—runs 4,284 words. The president of Columbia University, Nicholas Murray Butler, produced that whopper in his 1943 annual report. But *Columbia Magazine* said, "He was worse, however, when terse. His campaign slogan during the 1920 primary [when he was New York's favorite son]: 'Pick Nick for President and PicNic in November.' "[40]

George Will says, "Television news is the survival of the briefest."

"The Supreme Court has postponed the execution of convicted Texas murderer Jerry Yureck until the justices can consider his formal appeal. His electrocution was scheduled for Wednesday. He is in line to become the second criminal executed in the United States since 1967."

Somehow, "in line" seems out of line. Your sentence gives me a picture of a man standing in line waiting his turn. Perhaps this would work better: "And he would have been the second U-S inmate executed this week, after a 10-year gap in executions."

Another inmate had already been executed that week.

No need for *formal.* A legal appeal *is* formal.

"Two Americans face a potential death sentence should they be convicted of spy charges being lodged against them by the F-B-I."

If convicted, they face a death sentence, and it is potent (but not potential).

---

40. Richard M. Gummere Jr., "Have Speech, Will Travel," *Columbia Magazine,* October 1984, 29.

For broadcast purposes, the "if" clause should come first.

But if this story just broke or is fairly fresh, then the lead should go something like this: "The F-B-I has arrested two Americans on charges of spying for the Soviet Union."

Or "Two Americans have been arrested on charges of spying for the Soviet Union. The F-B-I arrested them in Los Angeles. . . ."

"Five American sailors are MISSING in Barcelona harbor after the launch they were riding in overturned. Seventeen U-S sailors and Marines are confirmed dead. Another 18 are being treated in a hospital. The American launch either collided with a Spanish freighter or overturned while maneuvering to avoid the freighter."

I objected to the writer's leading with the missing men *that* way, even if the deaths had been reported earlier. If earlier scripts had led with the deaths, I would take a new tack: "U-S and Spanish rescue crews are searching Barcelona harbor for five missing U-S sailors. They're unaccounted for in a boating accident that left 17 U-S sailors and Marines dead . . ."

If the story had not been previously broadcast, I'd write: "A U-S Navy boat overturned today at Barcelona, Spain, and 17 sailors and Marines died. Five sailors are missing. Eighteen other Navy men are being treated in a hospital. Their boat either collided with a freighter or was trying to avoid her and overturned."

If the deaths have already been confirmed, we know the men are dead. So there's no need to say "*confirmed* dead." All we need is *dead.* If I knew that the cause of death was drowning, I would have said *drowned.*

You're usually better off starting a story about an accident or disaster with action, not numbers. Then, count the casualties. (See p. 129).

"A founder of the Black September terrorist group, suspected of masterminding the massacre of Israeli athletes at the Olympic games in Munich, goes before an investigating judge Monday in Paris, where he was arrested."

Try to keep subject, *founder,* and verb, *goes,* as close together as possible. How about beginning this way: "A Palestinian suspected of planning the massacre of Israeli athletes is to go to court in Paris. . . ."? Or: "The alleged planner of the Munich massacre is to go to court in Paris. . . ."?

Short Words

(See *Fancy Words.*)

Since

"His lawyer says that the U.S. Attorney's office has now decided no prosecution is warranted in the case, since the consulting firm turned out to be a losing proposition from which Schneiders made no money."

"Since" = from then until now. The word needed in this sentence is "because." For anyone accustomed to the preferred definition of "since," hearing it the way it's used here is confusing.

Since writing that memo, I've run across a rule set down by the syndicated columnist James J. Kilpatrick:

"Do not, when it can be avoided, use 'since' in a casual construction. The problem here is that 'since,' like 'while,' telegraphs an instant connotation of time passing. The reader [and *listener*] launches into a sentence beginning, 'Since it rained,' and his inner ear tunes itself for a principal clause telling us what happened in the time span thereafter. His ear is thus affronted when the sentence concludes, 'we called off the picnic.' There is nothing wrong with 'because.' It is an honest timber, capable of bracing a sentence."

Another Kilpatrick rule relevant to broadcasters: "Never, as you hope for heaven hereafter, write that something 'remains to be seen.' This is the certain mark of the empty but portentous writer. He has run out of conclusions, if he had any to start with, and takes refuge in a cop-out. It has not occurred to him that beyond this particular split second, everything remains to be seen."

So What?

"In Manchester, England . . . 7 seamstresses died last night when fire trapped them on the top floor of a 4-story building in which they were working overtime. The fire occurred only about 100 yards from a building struck by a fire in May of last year. 5 people perished in that blaze."

The second fire is not worth mentioning.

I'd bet that the next morning's best newspapers were carrying front-page stories that were worthier of use in that network newscast than a fire 3,336 miles east of Manhattan—and eight months old.

The previous fire might be worth mentioning in that script if it were related to last night's fire or if the victims also were seamstresses. Or if it had occurred recently. Or if both fires had struck the same building. Or if all our listeners were Mancunians, as people in Manchester are called.

The writer might try to justify mention of the second fire on the grounds that the script was broadcast at 3 a.m., Eastern time, a slow time for news, and that the second sentence is better than dead air.

"A Japan Air Lines cargo plane carrying cattle crashed in Anchorage, Alaska, today . . . moments after its takeoff in foggy weather. A federal official at the Anchorage airport says all five persons aboard were killed . . . and that four of the bodies have been recovered."

The recovery of bodies in this story is extraneous. (Another story I ran across today mentioned that air traffic had been diverted to Elmendorf Air Force Base, which seems even extraneous-er.)

In print journalism, the practice of pouring in every last fact that you've dug up is called "dumping your notebook." The type of cargo isn't important. That story is about a cargo plane that crashed and five people who were killed. After the writer leads with cattle, which is strange, he doesn't even tell us what became of them. Did they walk away from the crash? Or were they barbecued?

Special

"There's a special reception today for people who let the Carter family stay overnight in their homes during the campaign."

Where everything is special, nothing is special.

Besides, usually people *invite* candidates, they don't just *let* them stay.

Superfluous Words

"People were handing beer out to anyone and everyone, kissing total strangers and shouting again and again."

"Total" is unneeded.

Also avoid "*perfect* strangers." No one is perfect. And no bystanders are innocent.

"The original Watergate burglars are asking President Ford to wipe their official slates clean."

"Original" is superfluous, unless you're contrasting them to imitators or impostors.

Wipe the slate clean is a cliché.

"Peking Radio says the fossils, some dating back 160-million years, mark the first time evidence of dinosaurs has been discovered in such a high-altitude area."

"Area" is unneeded if you make it "at such a high altitude."

"Pipeline companies within a given state could sell across state lines without federal price ceilings."

"Within a given state" is extraneous.

Although *extraneous* and *superfluous* are generally synonymous, meaning "beyond what is needed," *extraneous,* with the prefix *extra,* carries the meaning of something external or foreign. Perhaps I shouldn't have used them interchangeably, but I had no editor.

"Palestinian leader Abu Daoud said today in Algiers that he is not the mastermind of the 1972 Munich

Olympics massacre and is willing to testify on his innocence before a West German court. But Daoud—whose release by French authorities last Tuesday touched off those widespread protests—said that West Germany would have to guarantee his safety and make all arrangements through the Palestine Liberation Organization. A spokesman for the West German Justice Ministry, which had asked France to hold Daoud for possible extradition, reacted with skepticism to the offer. There was no comment by Israel.

Israel was not a party to Daoud's offer. Although Israelis were killed, the crime was committed in W. Germany. Mentioning the lack of comment from Israel does not impart any information and does not advance the story. Further, the lack of comment, as you know, is not the same as a "no comment." In any case, Israel's attitude is known, and I can predict their response. So the last line of this story is extraneous.

In the second sentence of the script, delete *those* before *widespread protests.* The sentence would mean the same.

"The long-distance lines from Plains, Georgia, to various overseas capitals will be busy in the week ahead."

Substitute "phone" for "long-distance." All calls to distant places are long-distance calls. There's no need to say, "I made a long-distance call to Fairbanks."

My memo went to an anchor, so I should have made that city in Alaska *Anchorage.*

"In below-freezing weather, this soldier on Capitol Hill is not waiting for a bus. He and hundreds more spent early Sunday morning rehearsing for Jimmy Carter's inauguration and the big parade afterward."

"Below-freezing" and "sub-freezing" are no colder than "freezing," just longer.

"Gonzalez says Sprague himself is becoming an issue, as seen in negative publicity about his past record as a controversial Philadelphia prosecutor who might trample civil liberties in his search for new facts about the Kennedy and King murders."

"Past" is unneeded.

What *is* needed in that script is a straightening out.

"As Secretary of State Vance escorted Dobrynin to his limousine, they reached agreement on a specific date for the Secretary's visit to Moscow next month, basically to launch a new serious effort to conclude a strategic arms agreement by this coming October."

Whatever is launched, usually (and preferably) ships, there's no need for "new."

Also superfluous: *specific* (a date *is* specific) and *this coming* (in a script written in February, the next October needs no *next*).

This script, too, needs a rewrite.

"And the Brazilians are planting more coffee trees, with prices higher than ever in history."

"In history" is superfluous.

"A Miami cruise ship is without power off the coast of Cuba, and the Coast Guard says the 352 passengers aboard the Monarch Star are being transferred in life boats to a sister ship, the Monarch Sun, which already has 409 passengers of its own but which can accommodate the extra people."

". . . off Cuba. . . ." suffices; "the coast of" is superfluous.

That was the least of the script's problems. With 52 words in one sentence, it's a maritime disaster.

"At pumping stations like this one, heavy demand has meant each trucker must wait in line for his turn, delaying delivery, sometimes for hours."

"For his turn" is extraneous.

We must guard against superfluous words, phrases and sentences.

Recent CBS scripts:

"According to witnesses on the scene, the plane developed some sort of trouble, descended to 11,000 feet . . . ."

A witness is someone who has seen or heard something, so where else would a witness be but *on the scene*? Also superfluous is *some sort of.*

"Two U-S Air Force F-15 fighter planes on training flights collided in mid-air today over West Germany near the French border . . . ."

If the crash occurred *over* someplace, it had to be *in mid-air,* wherever that might be.

"Among other things, Breeden was a key player in drafting the terms of the savings-and-loan bailout legislation."

Some writers have an affinity for *among other things,* apparently in the belief that it covers all bases, including home base. As used in that script, *among other things* could mean that Breeden was a key figure in drafting other bills or that his role in the S&L bailout was just one of his many activities.

Rookies rely on *among other things*: "Mayor Boodle said, *among other things,* he's going to overhaul city government." Or "The City Council acted on several matters today, *among other things,* the selection of a new leader." If any of those *other things* is worth mentioning, spell it out. But passing reference to *other things* tells us nothing.

Among other things beclouds a good story, as in this recent CBS News script:

"Among other things about the Justice Department, Congress is now investigating accusations of improper conduct by high-level Justice Department officials, including lying under oath in a case involving a multi-million-dollar Justice Department contract."

Among other things wrong with that sentence: Too many words (32), the Justice Department mentioned too many times (3), too many thoughts (4), too little thought.

Synonyms

"Spanish officials and American authorities today will attend a memorial service aboard the helicopter carrier Guam for the victims of last Monday's overturning of a launch bringing sailors and marines back from shore leave in Barcelona."

In the sense that you use "officials" and "authorities," I suppose you're using them as synonyms. O.K. But then why not write, "Spanish and American officials..."?

Today should be placed after *memorial service.*

The Fact That

"Egypt and Soviet Russia are glaring at each other again, this time as a result of last week's price riots in Cairo, Alexandria and other cities. President Sadat is blaming those riots on Communists as part of a plot to weaken Arab unity. Egyptian newspapers, going one step further, accuse the Kremlin of joining forces with Libya in a scheme to attack the Egyptian embassy in Tripoli, and they're publishing articles unfriendly to the Soviet Union. The Soviet news agency Tass, in quick response, charges that Cairo is trying to conceal the real reason for last week's rioting, which Tass says was an expression of popular indignation over Egypt's mounting economic troubles. Behind these polemics is the fact that Egypt is in debt to Soviet Russia to the tune of about five billion dollars in military and economic loans."

Problems, problems, problems.

The fact that should be deleted. The writer E.B. White called it a vile expression and said it caused his college English teacher, William Strunk, Jr., to quiver with revulsion. Their book, *The Elements of Style,* says *the fact that* "should be revised out of every sentence in which it occurs."

Soviet Russia? Nyet. Although many of us call the U.S.S.R. *Russia* and its people *Russians,* the *Soviet Union* and *Russia* are not the same.

Russia is the Russian Soviet Federated Socialist Republic, the largest of 15 republics in the U.S.S.R. *Soviet* refers to the system of governance. Using *Soviet Russia* as shorthand for the U.S.S.R. is akin to referring to this country as *Republican Alaska.*

Polemics is not an everyday word. Better: *argument.*

Is in debt to means *owes.*

To the tune of is a cliché.

This is a "new" script from CBS News, but the problems are old.

"First word that P-L-O leader Yasir Arafat was ready to talk despite the fact that the U.S. had refused him a visa came two weeks ago in a message from Sweden."

First, the objectionable phrase, *the fact that.*

What a relief to come to *came*! It's far too far from *first word.*

Here's a better beginning: "The first word that P-L-O leader Yasir Arafat was ready to talk came two weeks ago in a message from Sweden."

There Is/There Are

"There's a special hearing scheduled in Newark, New Jersey, Monday to determine if Ivan Rogalsky, a Russian immigrant, can afford an attorney. The New Jersey auto mechanic, who was arrested by the F-B-I, is charged with conspiring to pass secret documents to a Soviet diplomat, and has refused to answer questions about his financial status. . . ."

Save "special" for special occasions; it's overused.

The hearing was routine, but it needn't be labeled at all.

The script has more problems than the prisoner, except the writer can't go to the pen. First, the opening: "There is." It's a dead phrase. When a writer reads his script and finds he has started with "There is," he should delete those two words and insert an action verb. Why do so many writers start stories with "There is"? It's easy, and weak writers have a weakness for it.

If they're too weary to boil down their notes or their source copy, often a word-pudding, and they're stumped in writing a good, strong lead, they can always sit back and revert to flimsy old crutches, "There is," "It is" or "It was."

In the first sentence of the script, *if* should be *whether.*

His financial status? The diplomat's? That isn't what the writer meant, but that's what he wrote. Better than *financial status: finances.*

Stronger: "A hearing is scheduled in Newark, New Jersey, to decide whether a Soviet immigrant charged with conspiring to pass secrets to Moscow can afford a lawyer."

Let's look at some other recent CBS News scripts:

"It was a pitched battle today between left-wing demonstrators and Japanese police at Tokyo's International Airport. Hundreds were injured, hundreds arrested, in the protest against plans to expand the airport."

Pitched battle is a *strife-torn* cliché.

Better: "Hundreds of protesters in Japan fought with police against expansion of Tokyo International Airport." Yes, I left out *today. Today* and *tonight* do have their place in stories, but not every story, story after story. Too many writers use them indiscriminately. "They should be used sparingly, especially in the opening sentence," one early expert wrote. "The listener is under the correct impression that the news is all today's developments, so there is no need to put one in each story. The more desirable present tense normally obviates them anyway. You're not writing for a newspaper, so delete all except a very few."[41]

"There is apparently yet another spy scandal growing."

Better: "Another spy scandal seems to be brewing."

41. Burton L. Hotaling, *A Manual of Radio News* (Milwaukee: The Milwaukee Journal, 1947), 17.

"There aren't many people in Congress who list their previous occupation as basketball player. Bill Bradley is one of them."

Better: "Few people in Congress have been pro basketball players. Bill Bradley is one of them."

"There's no end of stories about how much and how deep the federal deficit is. Today, a report on how much is owed to the federal government in overdue debts."

How much and *how deep* sound like *one and the same.* Better: "The country has been running a surplus—on stories about how much the government owes. But today a report was issued on how much money the government is owed."

"There were burial services today across the nation for American soldiers killed in that Canadian air crash returning from the Sinai two weeks ago."

Better: "Funerals were held across the country today for U-S soldiers killed two weeks ago in a plane crash. The men were returning from the Sinai when their chartered plane crashed in Canada."

"There is economic aid on the way for the victims of last week's tornadoes."

Better: "Economic aid is on the way to the victims of last week's tornadoes."

"There were more spectacular pictures today of the planet Neptune and its moon Triton. They were made public as the scientists connected with the Voyager-2 project held their last news conference."

Better beginning: "More marvelous pictures of the planet Neptune and its moon Triton have been made public."

"There was a story published over the weekend that said a senior Soviet K-G-B officer had defected to the United States and is in the custody of the C-I-A . . . ."

Better: "A story published over the weekend says a senior Soviet K-G-B officer defected to the United States. The story—published in [name of publication]—says he's being held by the C-I-A."

The supply of these spongy leads is endless, but good writers avoid them. So there.

Thing

"It's not certain whether the cross-border movement is a one-time thing or represents the beginning of a general easing of tensions in the area."

The best things in life aren't things. Avoid them. *Thing* is vague. It's barely better than *thingamajig* or *whatchamacallit.* Find the noun that means something close to what you need. In that script, consider *event, affair, occurrence.* Or find an even better word and do your own thing.

You could write, ''It's unclear whether the border crossings reflect the start of an easing of tensions or are just an exception.''

Titles

"Claudine Longet, the singer-actress, went on trial today in Aspen, Colorado, charged with felony manslaughter in the death last March of professional skier Spider Sabich. If convicted, Miss Longet could face a maximum penalty of ten years in prison."

Broadcast style calls for the use of titles [or labels or descriptions] before names, unless you're writing about someone who enjoys instant name recognition. So it's better to say ''Singer Claudine Longet'' or ''The singer Claudine Longet.''

Manslaughter *is* a felony, so ''felony manslaughter'' is redundant.

Further, if convicted, she *would* face a prison term.

Try To

"The American Civil Liberties Union plans to file suit in federal court and in Utah State Court today to try and stop the execution of Gary Gilmore. Gilmore is scheduled to be executed by firing squad next Monday. Yesterday, the Supreme Court, in a one-sentence denial, refused a request to stay Gilmore's execution, a request filed by an excommunicated Mormon. There have been reports of protesters planning to storm the prison to stop Gilmore's execution, but the Salt Lake County sheriff called those reports 'baloney' and 'Eastern talk.' "

It's "try to stop."

The second sentence should start with *he,* not *Gilmore.* The third sentence needs help: "Yesterday, the U-S Supreme Court, in just one sentence, turned down a request. . . ." That deletes *denial.* And the reference to "one sentence" is expendable.

"One can only wonder what would have happened if a serious question had developed, which Mr. Carter would have found it in his interest to try and answer."

It should read, "try to answer."

And the script's *it* should be taken out.

"Next, if the weather permits it, Coast Guard divers hope to visit the sunken sections of the tanker to try and gather evidence for the inquiry."

"Try and. . ." is almost always wrong, "try to. . ." almost always right.

Unanswered Questions

"This is Malcolm X, the black nationalist leader of a decade ago. More than 10 years after he was assassinated, we now have learned that when Malcolm X was gunned down before a crowd in Harlem in 1965, one of his bodyguards was an F-B-I informer, who had penetrated the Muslim leader's inner circle. Witnesses tell us that the informer fell on Malcolm X as the shots rang out. Did the F-B-I know that Malcolm X was going to be assassinated? Did they know where and when? It was no secret that J. Edgar Hoover hated Malcolm X."

This item leaves the unsupportable implication that the FBI might have tolerated or even engineered Malcolm's murder. Malcolm and the Black Muslims had split acrimoniously, and the Muslims went to court to evict him from his home. The home had been provided him while he was their national spokesman. Three men were convicted of Malcolm's murder; two were Black Muslims. Through the years, [Black] Muslims have been involved in many crimes, often against one another. As newsmen, we shouldn't raise damning questions and let them hang there; we should get answers.

Did the FBI know of the impending murder? If so, did they know where and when? If they did, and the correspondent obtained proof, he'd have a story. And what a story! Instead, all he has are questions that sound like accusations.

The innuendoes spread by the correspondent are like those in a gossip column in a New York City tabloid:

"That was Ivana Trump who strode into 437 Madison Av. one afternoon last week—or it was a dead ringer. 'My girlfriend and I were having a cigarette near the bank of elevators that goes from the 22nd to 31st floors. It was definitely her,' said our source, a woman who works in the building. 'She was wearing a brown suit.' What makes this so intriguing is that Raoul Lionel Felder, one of the world's top divorce lawyers, has his offices on the 30th floor. 'What can I tell you?' Felder told us. 'No comment.' A few minutes later, he called back and said: 'She has not been here.' Donald and Ivana Trump both denied that she had been in Felder's office.''[42]

Eleven months after that item ran, the first hard news broke about the Trumps' marital problems. But that doesn't retrospectively justify using an item so wispy that it even gives gossip a bad name.

When you have tips, hunches and questions, all you have are reasons to start digging. But until you get the facts, you don't have a story.

My CBS memo died aborning because the committee that reviewed my work said the memo went beyond my turf as *writing* ranger.

Unhealthy

"There's more evidence today that Moscow is living up to the State Department's assessment of it as an unhealthy diplomatic post."

People are unhealthy; places are unhealthful.

Is that a distinction without a difference? Not if you're a careful writer. *Healthful* means ''giving health''; *healthy* means ''having health.''

42. Richard Johnson, ''Page Six,'' *New York Post,* March 9, 1989, 6.

Foods and climates can be healthful, but only living things can be healthy, except in idioms like *a healthy attitude, a healthy serving* and a *healthy skepticism.*

Unique

"The general assessment of the meeting: it was unique, a fine discussion, all sides satisfied."

There's nothing unique about this misuse of "unique." Try "unusual," if indeed it was so.

"What used to be known as the gee-whiz school of writing, and probably is now known as the switched-on school, is too much with us," according to *Winners & Sinners,* the in-house monitor of the *New York Times.* "It takes several forms," *W&S* says. "One is uniqueness ('the first of its kind'). Another, which closely resembles the first, is superlativeness ('The strongest speech yet,' . . . the most sweeping reform'). We even had a fleet of 41 ballistic missile submarines planned, developed and built 'in record time.' What was the previous record for this event?"

"San Francisco police are looking for a man who robbed a financial district bank in unique style. It all began in seemingly innocent fashion when a jogger entered a savings and loan office and asked for change of a five-dollar bill. The teller opened her cash drawer, and the man loosed a blood-curdling scream. The teller recoiled instinctively. Acting quickly, the man scooped up 11-hundred dollars, then left as he came, jogging, and melted into the sidewalk crowd."

"Unusual" is unusual enough. "Unique" would make it the only time ever. I wouldn't want to say that fellow's approach was unique, although I wouldn't hesitate to say it was unusual.

But I *should* have hesitated. I was too quick and too kind. That script has several other flaws:

What difference does it make to a listener in New England that the robbery was in San Fran's financial district? A savings and loan association is not a bank. (Recent scandals involving owners of S&Ls prompted one wag to quip, "How do you rob an S&L?" "Buy one." Another quipster: "What does 'S&L' stand for?" "Squander and loot." And let's not call anyone a *lone* gunman.)

Unless a robber shoots his way in, most bank robberies begin "in seemingly innocent fashion." And "seemingly innocent fashion" sounds suspiciously like a cliché.

The robber asked for change *of* a bill? Except in New York City, people request change *for* a bill or ask *to* change a bill. And only New Yorkers wait *on* line; other people wait *in* line.

"Blood-curdling scream" is a cliché. And "loosed" is a loser.

"Instinctively"? Eminently disposable.

"Acting quickly"? Would you expect him to dawdle?

An 11-hundred-dollar robbery, at least that one, is not national news for a network. That's petty cash. The robber should have been ashamed of himself. So should the writer. And the editor. And Mervin Block, too.

Unknown/Unfamiliar

" 'Transfiguration,' the last major work of the Renaissance master Raphael, has been returned to the Vatican museum in Rome after five years of restoration. Removed from the painting was a thick, two-century-old layer of yellow varnish, revealing vivid colors and detail. Art experts say this indicates, contrary to earlier belief, that Raphael did the entire painting, which was commissioned in 1517."

Broadcast style calls for holding back an obscure name. Ed Bliss, for one, says in Writing News for Broadcast: "NEVER start with a name that is unfamiliar to most listeners."[43]

This story is a tough one to write, but here's one possibility:

"The last major painting of the Renaissance master Raphael has been returned to the Vatican Museum after five years of restoration. A 200-year-old layer of varnish was removed, revealing vivid colors and detail on the canvas, titled 'Transfiguration.' "

My rewrite could use a makeover or, in the spirit of the canvas, a transformation. I'd change the second sentence to read:

"Removal of a 200-year-old layer of varnish has revealed detail and vivid colors. The canvas is titled 'Transfiguration.' "

In listing a series (*detail, vivid colors*), it's preferable to start with the short and go to the long or with the less important to the more important.

---

43. Edward Bliss Jr. and John M. Patterson, *Writing News for Broadcast* (New York: Columbia University Press, 1970), 41.

"Albert Finkley - 24 - of Fair Hope, Alabama - walked out of a federal institution in Texarkana, Texas, this evening - after having served three years. Finkley is news - because he is apparently the first man serving time for draft evasion - to be released from prison under today's pardon by the President. There are at least four others - now serving time. The White House estimates that Mr. Carter's pardon for draft evaders today - would affect hundreds of thousands."

Broadcast style calls for holding back an obscure name, not leading with it.

I should have also told the writer he gave the man's age in newspaper style, not broadcast style. (See *Age*.) And he should have used the word *prison* in the first sentence, not *institution*. Instead of telling us the man *is* news (whatever that means), the writer should have told us the news.

Better: "A federal prison in Texas released a draft evader this evening, apparently the first one freed by today's Presidential pardon. At least four other evaders are serving time. The White House says Mister Carter's pardon will affect hundreds of thousands of people. The man freed tonight is 24-year-old Albert Finkley of Fair Hope, Alabama. He had spent three years in prison."

"Dissident sources in Czechoslovakia say that secret police in that country have arrested at least six dissidents in a crackdown against publication of a charter on human rights. Said to be among those arrested was Jiri Hajek, a former Czech foreign minister. The report says one Czech writer and his wife were arrested and that the woman was seen being dragged into a car."

It would be better here to put the label before the name: ". . . a former Czech foreign minister, Jiri Hajek." That way, the listener would learn quickly that he's important.

Further, putting a title or a description *before* a name is broadcast style.

The first sentence should be tightened: "Dissident sources in Czechoslovakia say secret police have arrested at least six people in a crackdown against publication of a charter on human rights." No need for *that* after *say* and no need for *in that country.* Where else?

Upcoming

"The Japanese government this morning displays unhappiness over upcoming U-S regulations on foreign fishermen."

"Upcoming" is a barbarism. Try "impending," "approaching," "coming," etc. I can't tell whether any of these would fit in this instance, but I do know that "upcoming" is more appropriate for a cable.

In the old days, when print correspondents sent cablegrams, radiograms or telegrams, they tried to squeeze a lot of information into as few words as possible, even merging words, to *downhold* costs. For example, *Londonward* meant "I'm going to London," *scald* meant "so-called," *tany* meant "to any." And *upcoming* sounds like one of those telescoped words.

More than 30 years ago, the editor of the *Wall*

Street Journal sent a warning from his upstairs office to an underling: ''If I see 'upcoming' in the paper again, I'll be downcoming and someone will be outgoing.''

Vogue Words

"...and Peter Warg in Cairo tells us about the thrust of their discussions."

''Thrust'' is one of those vogue words thrust into bureaucratic reports. One of the nation's most pressing needs is an Anti-Thrust Act, according to Ed Newman, who inveighs against ''thrust'' in his Strictly Speaking. I, too, veigh in against it.

Other vogue words: *arguably, end-product, interface, operative, opt, prioritize, supportive, viable, wellness.* For *dialogue,* why not use, instead, *conversation, discussion* or *negotiation*? Or *talks*?

Weak Words

"The guns are active in southern Lebanon... Palestinians and Christians using artillery in the hills near the Israeli border."

''Using'' is weak; how about ''firing''?

"Using" has its uses, but when it comes to guns, *firing* is more precise and carries more firepower. But that writer misfired: he wrote a run-on sentence, two independent clauses joined improperly. His run-on sentence is called a comma splice; the clauses are joined with a comma but without a coordinating conjunction: *and, but* or *so.*

Try plain English: "The guns are active in southern Lebanon, and Palestinians and Christians are firing artillery. . . ."

Why didn't the writer use a comma, with one keystroke, instead of those three dots? Writers of books and articles (but not broadcast writers) use three dots (an ellipsis) only to indicate an omission of one or more words in a quotation. For lopping off the end of quoted matter, they use four dots—three for the omission and one as the period. For centuries, writers have relied on standard punctuation—commas for pauses, dashes for emphasis or pauses, colons for pauses, and periods for stops—and have made their mark without going dotty.

"Flags were at half-staff in Washington today in memory of Texas Congressman Mickey Leland and 15 others who died with him in a plane crash in Ethiopia."

Were is weak. Better: *flew* or *hung.* This recent CBS News script shows the weakness of linking verbs. Among them are all forms of *to be (is, are, was, were, will be), becomes, acts, seems, smells, sounds, tastes* and *looks.* A linking verb links or describes the subject of the sentence. It doesn't move. It doesn't act, and it doesn't express action. It just sits there.

"At the same time, wall posters have begun calling for the four radicals themselves to be executed, and some analysts feel execution is being seriously considered, at least by certain members of China's leadership."

"Feel" is weak; use "think" or "believe." Limit "feel" to dealing with fabrics or health.

Where

"There are still a few minor problems with Raymond Kurzweil's new machine. But, so what? The machine takes a book or a speech and—through a computer—it reads . . . out loud. It reads the Gettysburg Address, for example. It reads to the blind, long before some of the books it reads come out in Braille. Sometimes, it reads with an accent. Abraham Lincoln's words sound Scandinavian. But no matter. The computer's voice does not have a monotone. It has inflection and emphasis. And for all we know, it poses a terrible threat to people like . . . ."

Who's Kurzweil? What are those minor problems—or are they so minor they don't deserve mention at all? There's no *where* there. Where can I see the machine? Where can I hear it? Where is it made? And where can I find Kurzweil?

"A newspaper in Hong Kong reports that twice-purged Dung Siaow Bing has again been restored to favor—and named prime minister . . . . succeeding his onetime mentor, the late Jo en-Lai. The newspaper sez Dung has already begun his duties under Party Leader Hwa Gwo-Fung and that an official announcement's to be made later this month. The report cannot be confirmed. Dung was purged in the Cultural Revolution—then rehabilitated. Purged last April as a 'capitalist roader' by members of the so-called 'gang of four'—who have now been purged themselves."

Unless you read aloud the slug, the listener might be left in the dark as to the locale.

Although the script was slugged "China," listeners were never told where the story took place.

The writer should have inserted *but* before "The report cannot be confirmed."

Wire services lead their stories with datelines—date and place-name—but writers sometimes neglect to tell listeners the place-name. Not every story needs a "where." A story about the President or the U.S. Supreme Court needn't include Washington, D.C. But if the President speaks outside D.C., even outside the White House, the story needs a "where." Of that, writers should be aware.

"A cold windy night for the east has become a night of terror for a small New York town. A wind-whipped fire from a rubber manufacturing complex has set afire much of the downtown section of the village. Firemen were reported chopping through an iced-over reservoir to get to the water they need. Eyewitnesses spoke of exploding chemical and propane tanks. According to late word, the entire village of 17-hundred has been evacuated. No serious injuries reported—in Philmont, New York."

This script didn't lack a "where," but the "where" is in the worst place of all, at the end. It looks like an afterthought. (The writer, as a member of the American Federation of Television and Radio Artists, could call it an AFTRA-thought.)

Night of terror? *Terror* is excessive. Terror is intense, overpowering fear. No one is reported trapped or endangered, no homes damaged or threatened.

Wind-whipped sounds like wirese. (See *Journalese*.)

The script says firemen were "reported" chopping through ice. If the script was based on a wire service story, and most likely it was, there's no need for "reported." Write it as a fact. If the wire story said "firemen *reportedly* were chopping," find another way to say it. We shouldn't use "reportedly" if the information can be pinned down definitely. Either they were chopping or they weren't. There's a way to find out: phone a fire dispatcher or sheriff or state police, even a nearby newsroom. One of them is bound to know.

Perhaps "the late word" the script refers to arrived too late for a rewrite. But the story needs an updating: "A fire in upstate New York has caused the evacuation of an entire town—all 17-hundred people. But no one in Philmont has been reported hurt. . . ."

"The World Health Organization's hopes of declaring that smallpox became extinct in 1976 have been foiled by a new outbreak in Somalia. WHO officials say the outbreak in the Somalian capital of Mogadishu is the most frustrating of the decade-long global campaign to eradicate smallpox because single cases began popping up sporadically just when success appeared within grasp. The disease is believed to have been spread by nomads travelling from Ethiopia . . . reported last summer to be the last infected country in the world."

"Africa" should be inserted within the first few lines.

Foiled? Save it for a story about Dick Tracy's foiling bad guys.

Instead of *decade-long,* make it *ten-year.*

Extinct? That word usually applies to plants, animals or volcanoes.

Eradicate = wipe out.

Without the hyphenation of W-H-O so that the anchor reads every letter, he might—under the usual pressure and tension—inadvertently say "who."

"The London Press Association reports there's been a large volcanic eruption in eastern Zaire. The initial report speaks of at least two-thousand people killed."

Because Zaire is a fairly new state and our listeners are not cartographers, I think it'd be helpful to add "in Africa" right after "Zaire" or at the end: ". . . two-thousand people killed in the African state." The "Morning News" used the former method.

Don't start by quoting a long name, especially of an unfamiliar organization. (See *Unknown/Unfamiliar.*)

Do your maximum utmost, as the actor Edd "Kookie" Byrnes used to say, to find an action verb for the first sentence. If you don't have confidence in the account supplied by the London Press Association, probably to a U.S. wire service, try writing the story this way:

"A volcano in Zaire reportedly has erupted, and the word from the new African nation is that at least two-thousand people have been killed."

Whether Or Not

"The Palestinian leader who calls himself Abu Daoud is being held in a French prison while Israeli and West German government leaders try to decide whether or not to ask for his extradition."

"Or not" is unneeded with "whether" because "whether" means "whether or not."

Theodore M. Bernstein devised a test to tell whether there's need for *or not*: Substitute *if* for *whether*. If the change to *if* produces a different meaning, the *or not* must be supplied.[44]

Wordiness

"Clarence Mitchell, a veteran N-A-A-C-P official, issued a blistering indictment of. . . ."

This is a wordy way to say "denounced," "scolded," "scorched," "assailed," etc. Besides, it's a cliché.

"Today Senate Banking Chairman Wiliam Proxmire voiced criticism of Mrs. Harris's lack of experience in housing. . . and said that he might vote against her."

44. Theodore M. Bernstein, *The Careful Writer* (New York: Atheneum, 1968), 476.

"Voiced criticism of" is a long way to say "criticized."

And the script has no need for *that.*

"And one senator has given warning that Califano will be questioned about abortion."

Given warning = warned.

"Israel today made an official protest to France against the release of the Palestinian guerrilla leader, Abu Daoud. . . ."

"Made an official protest" = "officially protested" or "protested officially."

If it's not too late, I'd like to delete "officially." When one country protests to another country, it *is* official.

"Not far from Sydney, Australia, rescue teams are prying rescue victims out from under slabs of concrete, the remains of a 100-ton bridge which collapsed and flattened a commuter train, after it derailed. . . . Unconfirmed reports say as many as 80 people may have died."

"Not far from" = "near." The site was a suburb.

Easier to understand: "A bridge near Syndey, Australia, collapsed on a commuter train, and as many as 80 people reportedly were killed."

Die is a weak word. They did die; everyone who's killed dies. Most people die of illness or natural causes. A passerby might have died of a heart attack. But all those people presumably were *killed.*

"Foreign ministers of the European Common Market are conferring today in London. It's the first time they've met on British soil. Major items on the agenda, in addition to the issues that always concern the European trading community, are plans for a conference in Belgrade this summer on East-West relations, and the Rhodesia crisis."

"On British soil" = "in Britain."

The first sentence is typical of too many scripts: It sounds like an item that could have been written the previous day, the previous week or the previous month. Rather than write a bulletin-board item, it's better to say something that wasn't previously known.

"Violence is still sweeping the streets of Cairo tonight, despite government action to bring the riots to an end."

"Bring the riots to an end" = "end the riots."

"The Indiana Legislature has now approved the Equal Rights Amendment. . . .the 35th state to do so . . . .three more..and it becomes part of the Constitution. It was close in the Indiana state senate. If one senator had gone the other way, it would have been a dead heat. State Senator Wayne Townsend wasn't sure how he'd vote..was WAVERING..until he got a phone call that CONVINCED him to vote FOR ratification. That call . . .from Rosalynn Carter . . .First Lady ELECT."

Try "tie."

As long as the closeness of the vote is the focus of the story, why not tell us how many voted Aye, how many, Nay? Eh?

Instead of *Townsend wasn't sure,* make it *Townsend was unsure.*

I should have underlined *convinced.* You convince someone *that* you're right, or you convince him *of* the rightness of your position. *Convince* is followed by *that* or *of,* but not *to.* The word that should have been used is *persuaded.*

First Lady-*elect*? I don't recall seeing *her* name on the ballot.

"Bush said it would be improper to give his own personal view of the controversy over Theodore Sorensen, but the outgoing C-I-A director answering reporters' questions differed with Sorensen's statement that a substantial portion of the intelligence community is not yet ready to accept an outsider of his convictions as head of the C-I-A."

Delete either "own" or "personal."

Yes, that script is all one sentence: 54 words.

Instead of using the fancy *portion,* the writer could have said *part.*

Whenever I hear someone referred to as an *outgoing* officeholder, I think of an extrovert.

"*Of* his convictions"? Should be "*with* his convictions."

"Rejecting the idea of an unconditional Vietnam amnesty, President Ford instead relaxed some of the provisions of his original clemency program in order to upgrade the less than honorable discharges for some war deserters who were wounded or cited for valor. The plan was a disappointment to Mrs. Philip Hart, widow of the late Michigan senator, who had asked the President to grant general amnesty. . . ."

"Cited for valor" = "decorated."

And *widow of the late* is a redundancy.

"Omit needless words." That's the watchword Strunk and White stress:

"Vigorous writing is concise. A sentence should contain no unnecessary words, a paragraph no unnecessary sentences, for the same reason that a drawing should have no unnecessary lines and a machine no unnecessary parts. This requires not that the writer make all his sentences short, or that he avoid all detail and treat his subjects only in outline, but that every word tell."

Wrong Word

"At its best, democracy is a collusion between the hopes of the governed and limitations of their governors."

"Collusion" implies an act that's secret and sinister.

The writer probably meant *compromise.*

"One slim silver lining, though: it's less likely this morning that natural gas to private homes will have to be cut."

There may be various thicknesses of linings, but a silver lining cannot be slim.

It'd have to be thinner than *slim.* Even thinner than *thin.* All linings are, more or less, equally thinny-thin-thin. Only winter-wear linings are thick. If the writer is overcome by an irresistible impulse to qualify *silver lining,* she can use a word that probably comes closer to what she wants to convey: *slight.*

Less likely than what? Less likely than running across another cliché as threadbare as *silver lining*?

"It really wasn't a come-as-you-are party. It was more like a come-as-you-might-have-been back in the Middle Ages. You could hoist hippocras, spiced wine, just the way your forebearers might have done."

The word is "forebears."

Hippocras? That word shouldn't befuddle Jane and Joe Six-Pack. They'll be able to find it in their unabridged dictionary, the 15-pounder they keep on a teak stand next to their leather couch.

Perhaps the anchor made it clear, through his delivery, that *hippocras* was not the glass holding the wine, but I didn't hear him. He'd have removed all doubt if he had said, "hippocras, which was a spiced wine. . . ." Better yet, he could have left *hippocras* in the big dictionary, next to Hippocrates.

"And then the real fun began: trying to get close enough in the mob to catch a glimpse, to hear a phrase from the man they'd come to see. It was an insurmountable task."

It might have been extremely difficult, but I doubt that it was insurmountable. Even Everest is not.

"Mr. Carter will meet with the Joint Chiefs of Staff at Blair House for a close-up look at the military strength of Russia and other U-S adversaries."

No matter how detailed the data Carter may examine, I doubt that he'll get a "close-up" look at anyone's military strength, certainly not at Russia's.

Try: "Mr. Carter will meet with the Joint Chiefs of Staff today to find out what they know about Russia's military strength. And he'll also learn about other possible adversaries. The meeting will take place in Blair House."

"And for the last three months, the people of Salt Lake City and the rest of country have been witness to Gilmore's fight to get in front of the firing squad, despite the best efforts of well-minded civil libertarians to prevent it."

Mind your choices: try "well-intentioned" or "well meaning."

Better: "Gilmore has fought to get in front of the Utah firing squad, but civil libertarians have tried for three months to keep him alive."

"Amidst the Senate and House haggling over an emergency natural gas bill came growing charges today that the gas companies have been holding back production. Ohio Senator Howard Metzenbaum telephoned President Carter to inform him that he was sending this letter to the Interior Department, citing numerous examples of where natural gas supplies that are earmarked for nationwide distribution were not produced."

Amidst is an archaic form of *amid.* And you don't start a sentence with either of them. If *amidst* is used at all today, I suspect it's used only *amongst* monks.

While we're looking at that script, we should also see that it has other defects:

The past tense *came* should be the present tense *come.*

The use of a gerund (*haggling*) usually requires the noun preceding it to be in the possessive form: ''The Senate and House's haggling.'' But that sounds as though the two chambers are working as one, like in ''Gilbert and Sullivan's operettas.'' The House and Senate are separate bodies, so the script should say ''the Senate's and the House's haggling.'' But that sounds stilted, so I'd say, ''the haggling by the House and Senate.'' Or ''the haggling by Congress.'' ''Or Congress's haggling.'' But are they *haggling*? Maybe. But when I hear *haggle,* I think of tourists at a flea market or Mideastern merchants bargaining at a bazaar.

"Syrian troops evacuated the offices of six daily and one weekly newspaper."

''Evacuated'' is not good because it makes it seem that the troops caused the offices to be emptied. ''Departed from'' is better. Also, there's a word missing after ''daily.'' Make it read ''six daily newspapers and one weekly.'' Better yet,''seven newspapers.''

If that happens, it may be hard to find any made-in-California fruits and vegetables in the supermarket at any price."

Perhaps stars can be made in California, but not farm-grown products.

"He's an old colleague and friend of President Carter and hand-picked by the new President for the job."

"Chosen" and "selected" are better than "hand-picked," which is best left for the farm.

Better: "He's an old friend of the new President, and Mister Carter has chosen him for the job."

"The black majority has been demanding political control and waging a guerrilla war to get it."

Has the black majority been waging the guerrilla war? Or has it been waged by a small number?

"Ground-Hog Phil seemed a bit taken aback by the assemblance there, and not the least bit impressed by the honor of it."

Assemblance doesn't exist—except in that script. The writer meant *assembly* or *assemblage.*

But even if the correspondent had got it right, he was wasting time by covering ground-hog day. It's nothing but a stunt to publicize Punxsutawney, Pennsylvania. And the media fall for it every February 2.

How could the correspondent read the mind of the ground hog and tell that he was *a bit taken aback* and *not the least bit impressed*? The writer dug himself an escape tunnel with *seemed,* but the overall effect, especially for unsophisticated listeners, is that the ground hog is a prescient creature whose behavior may have some predictive value. Hogwash!

No listener ever learns a thing from the coverage, except about the standards of some newspeople. Isn't there something else going on in the world more worthy of our attention?

"They are two of the nation's most notorious mass killers. Gerald Stano and Ted Bundy together have been linked to nearly 80 murders. The stays of execution, the third for Bundy, the second for Stano, gives them at least 60 more days to try to overturn their sentences."

A more recent CBS script. They were not mass murderers. They did not herd a group of people into a garage and kill them. The two men were serial killers. They killed people in various places, one at a time.

Gives should be *give*.

"In the first week of his administration, Congressional leaders made known their dissatisfaction with the consultation between Capitol Hill and the White House, or more to the point, the lack of it. Carter sent up a quick peace signal: he got the message. But now the weight is on the Congress. Case in point: the President's request for emergency powers to deal with the natural gas crisis."

The *weight*? Sometimes in that context, we use *burden,* but not *weight.* At least, the writer should be credited for not saying, *The ball is in their court* or *The ball is on their side of the net.*

"In a speech to the National Press Club in Washington, Secretary of State Kissinger said that conditions for peace in the Middle East are better now than they've been for several years. He also dismissed the notion that the Soviet Union has gained military superiority over the U.S."

"Belief" or something similar would be better than "notion," which is a vague idea. Kissinger may try to put down such a belief as merely a notion, but some responsible men hold such a belief because of their analyses of intelligence data.

The opening clause of the script is of secondary importance, and the word *speech* sounds like something that's going to be boring. Likewise, mention of the Press Club isn't going to make people turn up the volume. Better: "Secretary of State Kissinger says conditions for peace in the Mideast are better now than they've been for several years. And he dismisses the belief that the Soviet Union has gained military superiority over this country. He expressed those views today at the National Press Club in Washington, D-C."

Zeugma

A useful collection of writing mistakes should extend from A to Z, so I'm adding a zeugma to the lineup. A zeugma is the use of a word to modify or govern two or more words though it fits only one of them.

Although I didn't run into any zeugmas at CBS News (other than a few members of Zeugma Delta Chi), I stumbled on one recently at a newswriting workshop:

"Little Asher weighed in at seven pounds, fifteen ounces. . .& a total length of 19 and three-quarters inches."

The verb is *weighed in.* The complement, which completes the meaning, is the weight, *seven pounds, fifteen ounces.* But the verb *weighed in* applies to weight, not length. What's missing is a verb that would fit *length,* perhaps *measured.* You can't say he *stands* 20 inches high. (In describing a newborn baby, the adjective *little* is superfluous. And *total length* is no longer than *length.*)

So let's rewrite it: "Asher weighs seven pounds, 15 ounces, and is 19 and three-quarter inches." That corrects the sentence by inserting *is,* shifts to the present tense, deletes *little, in, at* and *total,* gets Asher off to a good start and gives the author a fast out.

Many topics dealt with in this book are treated at greater length in a professional handbook, *Writing Broadcast News—Shorter, Sharper, Stronger.* Same author, same publisher, same message: Write to the point.

Appendix A

CBS MEMORANDUM

FROM: Emerson Stone
TO: CND, Radio, Personnel cc Richardson, Block
DATE: January 7, 1977

For a month or so, effective January 10th, Merv Block, whom many of you know from long and varied editorial associations with CBS News (broken by a spell as Professor of Journalism at the University of Illinois) will be on board again with us on an experimental basis as an Editorial Consultant.

His effort, through reviewing material already broadcast, will be to aid us all in raising the quality of our editorial product to an even higher level, on both the radio and television sides.

His is not to be a second-guessing or sniping-after-the-fact operation -- anything but. It <u>will</u> be, we hope, the contribution of a fresh pair of eyes (with even more experience in the practice and teaching of daily newswriting than most of us possess) to try to see ways we can improve how we communicate verbally. (This effort in the editorial area is intended to supplement the Pronunciation and Speech guidance we shall continue to receive separately from Richard Norman.)

Merv will work with us in two ways: first, with the luxury of time to reflect on material previously produced under deadline, he will communicate by memorandum specifically with those directly involved in a given broadcast or portion of a broadcast, when he has a thought that may be useful next time around; second, he will compile a weekly summary of his critiques for more general distribution.

As this experiment proceeds, I would welcome constructive thoughts on any aspect of it.

Appendix B

SECOND LOOK

CBS News No. 3

Honor detail. "And the new, informal President, wearing a tuxedo with a clip-on bow tie, moved briskly..."(Jan. 21, TV, Bruce Morton). Mention of the clip-on tie provides telling -
tail. Bruce also rates a salute for his farewell to Jerry Ford on the Morning News, Jan

Lend/loan. "And the airlines offered to loan 3,000 umbrellas..."(Jan. 20, T
airlines call themselves Loan Eagles, the verb needed here is "lend." "Loa

Overloaded. "Boats literally cannot move"(Jan. 21, TV). If boats ca
"Literally" adds only bulk.

Current events. "We'll have a report on current White House
rent energy problems"(Jan. 25, TV). Apparently, there's n

Hollywood's Vine? "If that happens, it may be har ... ab forces
vegetables in the supermarket at any price"(J ... 6). "Hopefully"
fornia, but not farm-grown products. ... used above.

(front)

3---Count 'em---3. "The semi-officia
of Egypt, Syria and Sudan will ... e switch into the 3 a.m.
With three parties meeting, ... ently just run to a tele-
"Summit" is overused; save ... he got the cue. CBS News beat
three persons together b ... ellent reporter. The spot should
... writing. I'm not even sure it was
Newswordy. "While ... , in this case, is grossly unfair."
other Cart ... ---David Jackson
(Jan. 5

... ess by playing golf..."(Jan. 21, Radio, Charles
... 4, Radio, David Culhane) merits a spot here.

... evacuated the offices of six daily and one weekly newspaper"
... ot good because it makes it seem that the troops caused the of-
... ed from" is better. Also, there's a word missing after "daily."
... wspapers and one weekly." Better yet, "seven newspapers."

... e here has not been a bed of roses for them, but they're hanging in there"
... eruse has soiled even "a bed of neuroses." "Bed of roses" might have been
... was first used, but now it's withered.

"They'd never be missed" list. "There won't be the usual shopping list that a President wants from Congress"(Jan. 12, TV). Please avoid "shopping list," "laundry list" and other shopworn phrases.

The tried becomes trite. "President-elect Carter had his first taste of being in Washington, D.C.'s limelight at..."(Jan. 20, Radio). Curtis MacDougall's Interpretative Reporting called "in the limelight" a cliché 40 years ago. The fly in the ointment is that clichés no longer evoke instant imagery, except of a weary writer. It's not true that one cliché is worth 10,000 pictures.

Mervin Block, 518/6, ext. 5666 2/4/77

(back)

Appendix C

TV VIEW

EDWIN DIAMOND

'Every Medium Needs Editors'

Editing tends to be a dirty word in television. Typically in television news organizations, an editor is someone who cuts film or videotape on demand. The title "managing editor" may actually belong to the head of the assignment desk. While these are key jobs, they are not normally occupied by people with power to say to a newsgatherer or a documentarian, "You haven't done it right."

The downgrading of editing and editors follows in part from the fact that television tends to be a star medium. Already, NBC's new "Prime Time Sunday" is being spoken of as "The Tom Snyder Show." Several recent pieces on "Prime Time Sunday" — a contentious report on DC-10 safety, an exploitive interview with Judy Blume, the author of books for teen-agers with explicit sexual themes — bear the all-thumbs prints of Synder's hyped-up style from the "Tomorrow" show. (For the record, Paul Friedman, the executive producer of "Prime Time Sunday," states that final decisions on stories are made by him, on occasion "in consultation" with Synder.)

In theory, there is nothing wrong with strong personalities in the the editorial process Bill Moyers plays a dominant role in every step of the production of "Bill Moyers's Journal," which has just completed a generally solid season on the Public Broadcasting System. It is, indeed, "*Moyers's* Journal." Yet, Moyers brings an experienced editor's news judgment and sensibility to the program. On Moyers's program, a moral issue may be joined with Garry Wills talking about Thomas Jefferson; on "Prime Time Sunday," the idea of a moral discussion involves two parish priests arguing about whether slain underworld figure Carmine Galante should be accorded a Catholic Church burial.

• • •

One restriction on editing in television is due to the limited amount of time available in a complex technology. Print reporters collect and write their stories and hand them to sub-editors who are paid to read through copy (or, nowadays, scan it on video display terminals). In television, one person may gather the story, a second person edit the film or tape, a third person prepare the script introductions and cues and a fourth person do the narration. The production process itself is so costly that it takes on an existence of its own; producers are likely to say, "Gee, think how we killed ourselves to get that footage. Let's use it." But the footage might not be appropriate, and often no one has the time to look carefully at how the parts fit. When the critics savaged the newsmagazine "20/ 20" after its premiere two seasons ago, ABC News president Roone Arledge, by way of defense, explained that he had prescreened individual segments but not the whole.

For almost 10 years now, in my role as an on-air commentator for news programs broadcast from Washington, D.C.,, I have been spending one day a week watching television newsrooms in action. Even in the best operations I have observed, the news director and the executive producer, serious professionals who were making prodigious efforts to supervise the preparation of copy and edited tape, still were. able to see the completed program for the first time only along with home viewers.

• • •

Another reason that television is under-edited derives from television's self-image, or what I think of as its self-deception. Some television producers, though certainly not all, really believe it when they say that the camera doesn't lie, or more sophisticatedly, that the camera can record the "real" reality — if only outsiders, kibitzers and anyone who wasn't there when the camera rolled would just stand aside. Such people often see themselves as documentary artists rather than broadcast journalists. The first generation of television journalists, such as Bill Moyers and Walter Cronkite and John Chancellor, came from newspaper or magazine backgrounds. The newer television generation tends to see itself as standing above and beyond print journalists with their fussy, too-literate regard for the facts and sober, non-hyped reportage.

The standards of print and of the traditional "serious" broadcasters, after all, seem quaint and old-fashioned to the new newsgatherers: They can do better. A year or so back, CBS News experimented with an in-house memo intended to take a second look at on-air news performance. The memo's author, the veteran journalist Merv Block, drew attention to details of grammar as well as to overall story effects, bestowing compliments as well as criticism. The CBS experiment in hindsight editing, admirable as it was, expired after just a few issues, reportedly because it stirred things up too much.

It is useful to look at two recent examples of under-editing in supposedly major-league television. Twice in the past year, the National News Council, a private foundation-funded group that investigates complaints about unfair or misleading journalism, upheld charges brought against two particular televised documentaries (the council has no power to punish, only to publicize its decisions). One complaint involved the independently produced "Bad Boys," first broadcast in October 1978 on WNET/Channel 13. The other involved the NBC News documentary "I Want It All Now," broadcast in July 1978. "Bad Boys" was produced for WNET by the husband-and-wife team of Alan and Susan Raymond. The Raymonds shot 80 hours of tape and edited this into a two-hour program, of which about 30 minutes focused on the students of Bryant High School in Queens. "I Want It All Now" was intended to be about life in Califor-

Edwin Diamond is a journalist and broadcast commentator. His latest book, "Good News, Bad News," was recently published by M.I.T. Press.

nia's Marin County. Both programs had an editorial point to make. "Bad Boys" looked at school truancy and its relationship to delinquency in later life. "I Want It All Now" was intended to show Marin County's laid-back, Cuisinart-and-hot-tub society, the landscape so deftly sketched by Cyra McFadden in her book "The Serial."

Without getting into the merits of the argument about the causes of delinquency or what may or may not be decadence in Marin County, it is possible to look at the complaints against these two programs and see how easily they could have been averted by a firm, knowing editorial eye.

For example, according to the council's report, the producers of "Bad Boys" spent several weeks at the Queens high school visiting various classes; yet, "Bad Boys" as broadcast concentrated on only one class — a typing class for problem students with learning difficulties. Students in crowd scenes outside the school were described as truants, though some were waiting to go to class or had finished class. As for "I Want It All Now," the program opened with an apparently nude woman, named Beth Furth, being stroked by peacock feathers wielded by two handsome young men at a massage service for women called Secret Garden. The program went on to quote figures about Marin County's 75 percent divorce rate, to characterize the Marin County suicide rate as twice the national average and to otherwise fill out the picture of overly indulgent, decadent "life styles." In fact, the Secret Garden scene was a "re-creation" of a massage Beth Furth had received in San Francisco, and the divorce and suicide figures were inaccurate. A questioning editor could have saved the Raymonds and NBC News the embarrassments of their mistakes.

As soon as someone suggests tough editing, others smell censorship and a challenge to relevant, strong television. Censorship and editing are not that hard to distinguish. There is no conflict between good television and good editing by editors so designated. "Bad Boys" was made by independents "in association" with WNET, and, just as independent producers are entitled to make their own documentaries, so too are station managements entitled to select, reject and supervise — in a word, edit — the programs they broadcast. Supervisory editors can't substitute their own viewpoints for those of the reporter or documentarian; no reputable print writer would allow an editor to do that, and neither should broadcast journalists. The main point, however, is that in every medium there is the need for an editor, a second pair of eyes.

More than two decades ago the broadcast team of Edward R. Morrow and Fred W. Friendly combined to produce excellent, and on occasion, highly courageous television programs. As Friendly recalls it, the collaboration of the star and the producer was built on the principle of editing. "There was a piece that Morrow never forgave me for when I wouldn't allow it to run," Friendly remembers. "But Ed and I could say no to each other and continue to respect one another and to work together."

That's the key: Editors are paid to say no. ■

Index

C

S

T

Y

Z